LIBRARIES OF THE FUTURE

LIBRARIES OF THE FUTURE

J. C. R. Licklider

THE M.I.T. PRESS
Massachusetts Institute of Technology
Cambridge, Massachusetts

SECOND PRINTING JULY 1965

COPYRIGHT © 1965 BY
THE MASSACHUSETTS INSTITUTE OF TECHNOLOGY
ALL RIGHTS RESERVED

LIBRARY OF CONGRESS CATALOG CARD NUMBER: 65-13831
MANUFACTURED IN THE UNITED STATES OF AMERICA

Foreword

THIS REPORT of research on concepts and problems of "Libraries of the Future" records the result of a two-year inquiry into the applicability of some of the newer techniques for handling information to what goes at present by the name of library work — i.e., the operations connected with assembling information in recorded form and of organizing and making it available for use.

Mankind has been complaining about the quantity of reading matter and the scarcity of time for reading it at least since the days of Leviticus, and in our own day these complaints have become increasingly numerous and shrill. But as Vannevar Bush pointed out in the article that may be said to have opened the current campaign on the "information problem,"

The difficulty seems to be, not so much that we publish un-

v

duly in view of the extent and variety of present-day interests, but rather that publication has been extended far beyond our present ability to make real use of the record. The summation of human experience is being expanded at a prodigious rate, and the means we use for threading through the consequent maze to the momentarily important item is the same as was used in the days of square-rigged ships.*

It has for some time been increasingly apparent that research libraries are becoming choked from the proliferation of publication, and that the resulting problems are not of a kind that respond to merely more of the same — ever and ever larger bookstacks and ever and ever more complicated catalogues. It was with this realization that the Ford Foundation in 1956 established the Council on Library Resources to assist in attempts to discover solutions to these problems and to bring the benefits of modern technology to the correction of maladjustments for which modern technology is to a large degree responsible. Somewhat later the Foundation earmarked a specific sum to enable the Council to concentrate its work in the storage and retrieval of information in a center involving the activities of specialized personnel.

Accordingly, early in 1961 the Council commenced a search for an appropriate site and for qualified investigators to undertake an inquiry into the characteristics of the "library of the future." In this search it consulted a number of persons especially thoughtful and knowledgeable in this nebulous area. Among them were Dr. William O. Baker, Vice-President for Research, Bell Telephone Laboratories; Dr. Lloyd V. Berkner, President, Graduate Center of the Southwest; Dr. Richard H. Bolt, Chairman of the Board, Bolt Beranek and Newman Inc.,

* Vannevar Bush, As We May Think. *Atlantic Monthly,* **176,** 101–108, July 1945.

and at that time also Associate Director for Research, National Science Foundation; Dr. Caryl P. Haskins, President, Carnegie Institution of Washington; Dr. Gilbert W. King, at that time Director for Research, International Business Machines Corporation, now Director of Research, Itek Corporation; Dr. Edwin H. Land, President, Polaroid Company; Prof. Philip M. Morse, Professor of Physics and Director of the Computation Laboratory, Massachusetts Institute of Technology; Dr. John R. Pierce, Director of Research in Communications Fundamentals, Bell Telephone Laboratories: Dr. Emanuel R. Piore, Vice-President for Research and Engineering, International Business Machines Corporation; Dr. Earl P. Stevenson, then Chairman, since Consultant, Arthur D. Little, Inc.; and Dr. Warren Weaver, Vice-President, Alfred P. Sloan Foundation.

There is perhaps no question that makes more instant demand upon the combined experience and imagination of the respondents, or as a result more widely differentiates one response from another, than does the question, "How should one explore the library of the future?" In this matter, too, the pattern was set by Dr. Bush in his 1945 article, to which reference has already been made, in which he invented the "Memex," the private memory device in which all a man's records may be stored, linked by associative indexing and instantly ready for his use. Just so, in its consultations the Council received as many answers as the number of persons whom it questioned, each answer widely different from the last: from one, an exhortation to investigate the fundamental processes of cognition; from another, an admonition on the importance of building consecutively from things as they are to things as they may be; from a third, a case history demonstrating the essential role of serendipity in the solution of difficult problems.

In one particular and only one was there agreement among the consultants: find the right man. And more and more frequently, as the consultations proceeded, the name of an individual emerged.

Dr. J. C. R. Licklider was at that time the supervisory engineering psychologist of Bolt Beranek and Newman Inc. of Cambridge, Massachusetts, consulting engineers with a primary interest in acoustics. (Dr. Licklider had been President of the Acoustical Society of America in 1958.) Behind him, at Harvard and the Massachusetts Institute of Technology, Dr. Licklider had left an enviable record of research on problems of human communication and the processing and presentation of information. This combination of training and experience seemed to the Council to offer an admirable background from which to prospect the "library of the future." On his side, Dr. Licklider was attracted by the problem and almost overnight wrote an eloquent prospectus for the first year's work. This, with very slight revision, was adopted, and the study commenced in November 1961.

In October 1962, Dr. Licklider took a year's leave of absence from Bolt Beranek and Newman on a special assignment for the Department of Defense. However, the "research on concepts and problems of libraries of the future" continued under his general direction in his absence. But when the year came around again it was not found possible to extend the relationship, and the study was brought to an end with the rendition, in January 1964, of the final report upon which the present volume is based.

The reader will not find here that a bridge has been

completed from things as they are to things as they may be, but he will find a structure on which he can take some steps out from the here and now and dimly descry the may be on the other side.

VERNER W. CLAPP

Council on Library Resources, Inc.
Washington, D. C.
August 1, 1964

Preface

THE STUDY on which this report is based was sponsored by the Council on Library Resources, Inc., and conducted by Bolt Beranek and Newman Inc., between November 1961 and November 1963. I acknowledge with deep appreciation the contributions of inspiration, thought, fact, and effort made by members of the two organizations.

The Council on Library Resources defined the general scope of the work and maintained, through its officers and staff and a special Advisory Committee, a spirited interaction with the contractor's group. I offer special thanks to Verner W. Clapp, President of the Council, Melville J. Ruggles, Vice-President, and Laurence B. Heilprin, Staff Scientist, for frequent infusions of wisdom and knowledge. The Chairman of the Advisory Committee, Joseph C. Morris, was a vigorous activator and a source of much encouragement. To him and to the members of the Committee — Gilbert W. Chapman, Caryl P. Haskins, Barnaby C. Keeney, Gilbert W. King, Philip M. Morse, and John W. Pierce — and to Lyman H. Butterfield, who was closely associated with the Committee, I express appreciation for a rare blend of administrative guidance and constructive technical criticism.

The colleagues within Bolt Beranek and Newman who participated most actively in the library study were Fisher S. Black, Richard H. Bolt, Lewis C. Clapp, Jerome I. Elkind, Mario Grignetti, Thomas M. Marill, John W. Senders, and John A. Swets (who directed the research during the second year of the study).

John McCarthy, Marvin Minsky, Bert Bloom, Daniel G. Bobrow, Richard Y. Kain, David Park, and Bert Raphael of the Massachusetts Institute of Technology were also part of the research group. The opportunity to work with those BBN and M.I.T. people was exciting and rewarding. I am appreciative of their comradeship and their contributions. I hope that I have done fair justice to their ideas and conclusions in Part II, which summarizes the individual researches that comprise the study.

Perhaps the main external influence that shaped the ideas of this book had its effect indirectly, through the community, for it was not until Carl Overhage noticed its omission from the References that I read Vannevar Bush's "As We May Think" (*Atlantic Monthly,* **176,** 101–108, July 1945). I had often heard about Memex and its "trails of references." I had hoped to demonstrate Symbiont to Dr. Bush as a small step in the direction in which he had pointed in his pioneer article. But

I had not read the article. Now that I have read it, I should like to dedicate this book, however unworthy it may be, to Dr. Bush.

J. C. R. LICKLIDER

Mt. Kisco, New York
November 4, 1964

Contents

CONTENTS

Introduction

FOR TWO YEARS *beginning in November 1961, a small group of engineers and psychologists at Bolt Beranek and Newman Inc. explored "concepts and problems of libraries of the future" under the sponsorship of the Council on Library Resources. This is a summary report of the study. It has two main parts. If the phrases were not so long, the parts would be entitled: (1) Concepts and Problems of Man's Interaction with the Body of Recorded Knowledge, and (2) Explorations in the Use of Computers in Information Storage, Organization, and Retrieval.*

SCOPE

The "libraries" of the phrase, "libraries of the future," may not be very much like present-day libraries, and the

1

term "library," rooted in "book," is not truly appropriate to the kind of system on which the study focused. We delimited the scope of the study, almost at the outset, to functions, classes of information, and domains of knowledge in which the items of basic interest are not the print or paper, and not the words and sentences themselves — but the facts, concepts, principles, and ideas that lie behind the visible and tangible aspects of documents. The criterion question for the delimitation was: "Can it be rephrased without significant loss?" Thus we delimited the scope to include only "transformable information." Works of art are clearly beyond that scope, for they suffer even from reproduction. Works of literature are beyond it also, though not as far. Within the scope lie secondary parts of art and literature, most of history, medicine, and law, and almost all of science, technology, and the records of business and government.

EPOCH

The "future," in "libraries of the future," was defined at the outset, in response to a suggestion from the Council, as the year 2000. It is difficult, of course, to think about man's interaction with recorded knowledge at so distant a time. Very great and pertinent advances doubtless *can* be made during the remainder of this century, both in information technology and in the ways man uses it. Whether very great and pertinent advances *will* be made, however, depends strongly on how societies and nations set their goals. Moreover, the "system" of man's development and use of knowledge is regenerative. If a strong effort is made to improve that system, then the early results will facilitate subsequent phases of the effort, and so on, progressively, in an exponential crescendo. On the other hand, if intellectual processes and their technological bases are neglected, then goals that could have been achieved will remain remote, and proponents of their achievement will find it difficult to disprove charges of irresponsibility and autism.

The remoteness of the planning target date, nevertheless, had a desirable influence on our thinking. It made it impossible to accept tacitly the constraints that tend to be imposed upon imagination by the recent course and current trend of technology. It freed us to concentrate upon what man would like the nature of his interaction with knowledge to be. That is possibly an important freedom, for extrapolation of the main courses of present-day library science and information technology does not lead to concepts or systems that seem either very desirable or very effective.

The Role of Schemata

Freedom from constraints imposed by existing concepts and devices, however, is double-edged. According to the most advanced theories of cognition, men think by manipulating, modifying, and combining "schemata." A new concept is achieved, not by creating a new schema *ab initio,* on a custom basis, but by adapting an old schema or, if necessary, arranging several refurbished schemata into a new, complex structure. If we renounce schemata derived from experience with existing library systems, file rooms, and computer centers, therefore, we have to be careful not to leave ourselves without parts from which to construct new concepts. A guideline for avoiding that predicament is to discard the upper-echelon

3

schemata — those at the level of system and subsystem — and to retain, for possible alteration and reuse, the lower-echelon, component-level schemata.

It is not possible, in a summary report, to present a complete inventory of promising component-level schemata, but it may be helpful to illustrate the idea of discarding schemata at the system and subsystem levels while retaining those at the component level. The illustration will take the form of comments about pages (components), books (subsystems), and libraries (systems).

PAGES, BOOKS, AND LIBRARIES

As a medium for the display of information, the printed page is superb. It affords enough resolution to meet the eye's demand. It presents enough information to occupy the reader for a convenient quantum of time. It offers great flexibility of font and format. It lets the reader control the mode and rate of inspection. It is small, light, movable, cuttable, clippable, pastable, replicable, disposable, and inexpensive. Those positive attributes all relate, as indicated, to the display function. The tallies that could be made for the storage, organization, and retrieval functions are less favorable.

When printed pages are bound together to make books or journals, many of the display features of the individual pages are diminished or destroyed. Books are bulky and heavy. They contain much more information than the reader can apprehend at any given moment, and the excess often hides the part he wants to see. Books are too expensive for universal private ownership, and they circulate too slowly to permit the development of an efficient public utility. Thus, except for use in consecutive reading — which is not the modal application in the domain of our study — books are not very good display devices. In fulfilling the storage function, they are only fair. With respect to retrievability they are poor. And when it comes to organizing the body of knowledge, or even to indexing and abstracting it, books by themselves make no active contribution at all.

If books are intrinsically less than satisfactory for the storage, organization, retrieval, and display of information, then libraries of books are bound to be less than satisfactory also. We may seek out inefficiencies in the organization of libraries, but the fundamental problem is not to be solved solely by improving library organization at the system level. Indeed, if human interaction with the body of knowledge is conceived of as a dynamic process involving repeated examinations and intercomparisons of very many small and scattered parts, then any concept of a library that begins with books on shelves is sure to encounter trouble. Surveying a million books on ten thousand shelves, one might suppose that the difficulty is basically logistic, that it derives from the gross physical arrangement. In part, of course, that is true, but in much greater part the trouble stems from what we may call the "passiveness" of the printed page. When information is stored in books, there is no practical way to transfer the information from the store to the user without physically moving the book or the reader or both. Moreover, there is no way to determine prescribed functions of descriptively specified informational arguments within the books without asking the reader to carry out all the necessary operations himself.

We are so inured to the passiveness of pages and books that we tend to shrug and ask, "Do you suggest that the document read its own print?" Surely, however, the difficulty of separating the information in books from the pages, and the absence, in books, of active processors, are the roots of the most serious shortcomings of our present system for interacting with the body of recorded knowledge. We need to substitute for the book a device that will make it easy to transmit information without transporting material, and that will not only present information to people but also process it for them, following procedures they specify, apply, monitor, and, if necessary, revise and reapply. To provide those services, a meld of library and computer is evidently required.

Let us return now to the problem of schemata from which to construct future systems to facilitate man's interaction with transformable information. As a shorter term for such systems, let us use "procognitive systems." * In thinking about procognitive systems, we should be prepared to reject the schema of the physical library — the arrangement of shelves, card indexes, check-out desks, reading rooms, and so forth. That schema is essentially a response to books and to their proliferation. If it were not for books, and for the physical characteristics of

---

* "Procognitive systems" is also more appropriate than "library systems of the future" to designate the objects of our study. "Systems" has, for us, the proper connotations. "Future" is correct, but it should not be necessary to repeat it explicitly throughout the discussion. The systems in which we are interested are broader than present-day libraries; the systems will extend farther into the process of generating, organizing, and using knowledge. Moreover, since the idea of "book" is not likely to be central, it seems best to substitute another word for "library." Since the systems are intended to promote the advancement and application of knowledge, they are "for knowledge," and thus *procognitive systems*. When this term is used in the plural, it refers to specialized systems as well as to the general, neolibrary system, and sometimes to successive generations of such systems. When it is used in the singular, it refers to the neolibrary system of the assumed epoch.

books that we have discussed, there would be no *raison d'être* for many parts of the schema of the physical library.

At the level of subsystem, we should be prepared to reject the schema of the physical book itself, the passive repository for printed information. That involves rejecting the printed page as a long-term storage device, though not for short-term storage and display.

At the component level, on the other hand, there are few library and documentation schemata that we should wholly reject, and many that we should retain. In addition to the schema of the printed page, we should retain schemata corresponding, for example, to:

1. Hierarchies of segments of text, such as the hierarchy of character, word, . . . sentence, paragraph, . . . chapter, . . . volume. . . .

2. The concepts of textual, tabular, graphical, and pictorial information.

3. Such concepts as title, author, abstract, body, footnote, and list of references.

4. Such concepts as original article, review article, note, letter, journal, and book.*

5. Such concepts as catalogue, index, descriptor, Uniterm, and thesaurus.

Although the foregoing constitutes a much abbreviated and perhaps only suggestive discussion of the relation of existing libraries to future procognitive systems, it may serve as an introductory clarification of the notion of selective retention of schemata for use in planning. The same notion is applicable to documentation centers, spe-

---

* In the sense of classes of information, not physical carriers of information.

cialized information storage and retrieval systems, and digital computing centers. A few remarks about digital computing centers will bring this topic to a close.

THE RELEVANCE OF DIGITAL COMPUTERS

The over-all plan of organization of the typical university or business computing center does not provide a good system schema for our purposes. If one thinks of "computing" in terms of collecting data and writing a computer program, having the data and program punched into cards, delivering the cards to a computer center in the morning, and picking up a pile of "printouts" in the afternoon, and so forth, he is likely to scoff at the idea that the science and technology of computing provide a large fraction of the extant ideas that are relevant to, and promising for, future procognitive systems. On the other hand, if one looks at the echelon below that of the computing center, he finds many promising schemata among the concepts, techniques, and devices. The most valuable are, by and large, the most abstract, and even those that are highly abstract may require much modification to fit into a system schema of the kind that we require. Almost surely, however, some of the information-processing schemata suggested by the following will play a role in shaping future procognitive systems:

1. Random-access memory,
2. Content-addressable memory,
3. Parallel processing,
4. Cathode-ray-oscilloscope displays and light pens,
5. Procedures, subroutines, and related components of computer programs,

6. Hierarchical and recursive program structures,
7. List structures,
8. Procedure-oriented and problem-oriented languages,
9. Xerographic output units,
10. Time-sharing computer systems with remote user stations.

What is of value for our purpose is not, for example, the oscilloscope or the light pen. It is the schema in which a man sits at a desk, writes or draws on a surface with a stylus, and thereby communicates to a programmed information processor with a large memory. It is the mental image of the immediate response, visible on the oscilloscope, through which the computer acknowledges the command and reports the consequences of carrying it out — in which the computer acknowledges the question and presents an answer. Without such schemata in mind, one cannot think effectively about future systems for interaction with the body of knowledge. With such schemata, and enough others suggested by experiences in other contributory fields, perhaps conceptual progress can be made.

It is important to recognize that our progress must, for a time, be largely conceptual or demonstrational. Present-day information-processing machinery cannot process usefully the trillions of bits of information in which the body of knowledge is clothed (or hidden), nor can it handle significant subsets efficiently enough to make computer processing of the textual corpus of a field of engineering, for example, useful as a tool in everyday engineering and development. The things of interest that the present computers can do usefully are (1) process data in experimental studies, and (2) simulate and demonstrate techniques and systems which, although they cannot yet be implemented fully, can be set forth in a dynamic form that is sufficiently realistic to facilitate evaluation and further investigation. The latter seems to us to be a particularly promising pursuit.

PART I

MAN'S INTERACTION
WITH RECORDED KNOWLEDGE

Our examination of concepts and problems in the domain of procognitive systems dealt with four topics:

1. *Information measures of the world's store of knowledge.*
2. *Aims, requirements, criteria, and plans for procognitive systems.*
3. *Schemata for storage, organization, retrieval, and dissemination of information.*
4. *Man-computer interaction in procognitive systems.*

The main lines of study, and the projections and conclusions to which they led, are set forth in the following chapters.

CHAPTER ONE

The Size of the Body
of Recorded Information

Estimates of the Size

As a basis for thinking about procognitive systems, one needs an estimate of how much information there is to cope with. The concepts — information measure and informational redundancy — are subtle; the simplest estimate needed is not. The simplest estimate needed is the number of alphanumeric characters that would be required to spell out the contents of all the documents in the libraries of the world, each document "type" (as opposed to document "token," or individual copy) being considered only once. An adjustment would have to be made to take into account pictures and other nonalphanumeric contents. Answers would be determined for such questions as, "Does translation from one language to an-

13

other create a new document type?" Various subdivisions of the total into parts are of interest. Even with those qualifications, however, the question of the total number of characters in the corpus is fairly simple and direct.

If a definite number of "bits" is assigned to each alphanumeric character, it is possible to multiply the total number of characters by the number of bits per character and say something like: "There are n bits of recorded information in the world's libraries." Or "It would take n cells of binary storage space to hold one copy of each document in all the world's libraries." The second statement seems preferable to the first. It is not clear, however, that converting from characters to bits offers any advantage other than the adventitious one of reconciling two estimates made in the course of our study.

During the first few months, a very rough estimate was made (Licklider, 1962), based mainly on the work of Bourne (1961) and on the size of the Library of Congress, together with some miscellaneous impressions. The first estimate gave $2 \cdot 10^{14}$ characters or (at 5 bits per character) 10^{15} bits.* Later, Senders (1963), after a much more careful study, estimated that the total lies between $3.8 \cdot 10^{13}$ and $3.8 \cdot 10^{14}$ characters or (at 12 bits per character) between $4.6 \cdot 10^{14}$ and $4.6 \cdot 10^{15}$ bits. The difference between the assumptions about exploitation of redundancy in the coding of characters (5 or 6 versus 12 bits per character), together with the round-off, almost exactly compensates for the difference between the estimates of the number of characters.

For our purposes, there is no need to resolve such

* Six bits per character was the initial assumption. In $6 \cdot 2 \cdot 10^{14} = 1.2 \cdot 10^{15}$, however, there is an unwarranted appearance of precision. We therefore used 5 bits per character as a temporary expedient.

"small" discrepancies. Let us merely average Senders' bounds and conclude that there are roughly 10^{14} characters and 10^{15} bits in the total store. The size of the store is doubling every 15 or 20 years, which makes the current growth rate about $2 \cdot 10^6$ bits per second (Senders, 1963). We might make the working assumption that there will be $2 \cdot 10^{15}$ bits in 1980 and $5 \cdot 10^{15}$ bits in the year 2000.

If we accept 10^{15} bits as the present total, then we may take about 10^{14} as the number of bits required to hold all of science and technology, and 10^{13} for "solid" * science and technology. Then, if we divide science and technology into 100 "fields" and 1000 "subfields," we come out with 10^{11} bits for a field, on the average, and 10^{10} bits or a billion characters for a subfield.

To relate the foregoing estimates to common experience, we may start with a printed page. If we assume pages with 100 characters per line and 50 lines, we have 5000 characters per page. Then, assuming 200 pages per book, we have 10^6 characters per book. Thus the "solid" literature of a subfield is the equivalent of a thousand books, and the total literature of a subfield is the equivalent of ten thousand books. If one thinks of information theory or psychophysics as a subfield, the figures seem not to violate intuition.

Size of the Corpus versus
Capacity of Computer Memories
and Speed of Computer Processors

One of the main prerequisites for effective organization of the body of knowledge is — if we may anticipate

---

* "Solid" is intended to delimit the literature by excluding popularizations, ephemeral items, and contributions from unqualified sources.

a conclusion to be developed later — to get the corpus, either all at once or a large cluster at a time, into a processible memory. How, then, do the estimates set forth in the foregoing section compare with estimates of the computer's memory size, both present and future? And how do estimates of the computer's processing capability compare with estimates of the amount of processing that would have to be done to organize the body of knowledge broadly and deeply?

Access to information requires time. Usually, two or more different "access times" must be considered. Even if one knows precisely the location of a passage that he wishes to read, it ordinarily takes a relatively large amount of time to get to the beginning of it. Thereafter, one can move from word to word within the passage at a rapid rate. That is to say, initial access time is ordinarily much longer than intraserial access time. That is the case for several kinds of computer memory, for example, magnetic tapes, magnetic drums and disks, delay-line memories of all types. A few kinds of computer memory, however, have only one access time: magnetic-core memories, thin-film memories, and certain cryogenic memories. They are called "random-access" memories because one may jump around from register to register at random just as fast as he can jump from a register to its nearest neighbor. The access time of widely used random-access memories is of the same order as the intraserial access time of serial memories, and very much shorter than the initial access time of serial memories. If the ratio of the incidence of initial accesses to the incidence of serial accesses is not extremely low, therefore, random-access memories offer an important advantage in speed over serial memories. In the kind of processing that is required to organize the body of knowledge, the incidence of initial accesses will be high. It is necessary, therefore, to consider random-access memories and serial memories separately, keeping it in mind that our purpose may be impossible to accomplish as long as the only very large memories are serial memories.

Fast random-access memories were unknown before World War II. A hundred 50-bit words is the largest capacity that existed two decades ago. Even as late as 1952, when the SAGE System* was being designed, it was difficult to provide 2000 fast, random-access words in a single computer memory, and it took the timely invention of the magnetic-core memory a decade ago to make "semi-automatic air defense" feasible. Now, the largest random-access memory holds about 130,000 words, which is approaching 10^7 bits. If the technology of magnetic thin-film memories is developed during the next few years in a way that now seems possible, we may have hundred-million-bit "modules," and several or many modules per memory, well before 1970.†

The brief course of development just summarized does not provide a firm base for extrapolation. However, the technology of digital memory is not operating near any fundamental physical limit, and new departures could continue to appear once every decade. The size of the largest fast, random-access memory could continue, on the average, to double every two years. If memory capacity were to grow at that rate, it would be possible to put

* Semi-Automatic Ground Environment System for Air Defense.
† Shortly after the text was written, "bulk core" memories, with 18 million bits per unit, and as many as four units per computer, were announced for delivery in 1966. A modern maxim says: "People tend to overestimate what can be done in one year and to underestimate what can be done in five or ten years."

17

all the solid literature of a subfield of science or technology into a single computer memory in 1985. The corresponding date for a field would be 1988 or 1989, and for all solid science and technology it would be about 1996. All this refers to fast, random-access digital memory.

How fast? There is little basis for expecting a marked increase in speed (and consequent decrease in access time) in the memories that are specialized toward maximizing capacity. Although low-capacity memories may become very much faster, only an optimist would hope for access shorter than 0.1 microsecond in the memories discussed in the preceding paragraphs.

The serial * memories that are of greatest interest in the context of this discussion are disk files and photographic memories. In the present state of the art, serial memories are much more voluminous than random-access memories. There are now available magnetic disk files that will store more than a billion bits. In testimony before a committee of the House of Representatives in 1963, E. R. Piore of I.B.M. said that his company was working on a trillion-bit photographic memory. For a rough rule, one might say that serial memories are ahead of random-access memories in capacity by a factor somewhat greater than 1000, behind random-access memories in initial-access speed by a factor considerably greater than 10,000, and almost even with random-access memories in speed of intraserial access. Advances in serial-access memory appear to be taking place somewhat more

* Disk files and some photographic memories — e.g., the "photoscopic disk" — are, from a technical standpoint, not precisely serial; rather, they are "cyclic." However, the distinction is not important to the present discussion. Magnetic tapes are serial, but handling tape introduces a third kind of access delay. Both access to a randomly selected tape and access to a randomly selected segment of a given tape are very slow.

18

rapidly than advances in random-access memory, but extrapolation into the distant future seems even less certain. Nevertheless, it is likely that within a few years it will be possible to fit the solid text of a subfield of knowledge into a serial memory. This focuses attention on the question, shall we then be able to process the text in a significant way, or shall we have to wait until we can at any moment achieve fast access to any part of the text?

Before examining what one should mean by "processing the text in a significant way," let us take one more look at a technological constraint — the constraint on "amount of processing." In computers of the type that are in widespread use today, one processor performs successive operations on the contents of memory. The operations correspond to "instructions" selected from a set, usually larger than 100. The fastest present-day machines execute about a million such instructions per second. The most promising technological paths appear to be open as far as 10 million, or perhaps even 100 million, instructions per second. Moreover, the idea of using several or many processors simultaneously — "in parallel" — is under active exploration and development.

Thus, one can look forward with reasonable confidence to a time when it will be possible to perform tens or hundreds of millions of operations per second upon the corpus of a subfield, or even a field, of the body of knowledge. That prospect supports the assumption, set forth in the introduction, that our thinking and planning need not be, and indeed should not be, limited by literal interpretation of the existing technology. Extrapolation, however uncertain, suggests that the basic "mechanical" constraints will disappear: Although the size of the body of knowledge, in linear measure of printed text, is almost astronomical (about 100,000,000 miles), although that measure is increasing exponentially, and although the technology that promises to be most helpful to us in mastering knowledge is still young and weak, time strongly favors the technology. The technology, too, is growing exponentially and its growth factor is perhaps 10 times as great as the growth factor of the corpus. Moreover, the technology is not yet near any fundamental physical limits to development. Thus in the present century, we may be technically capable of processing the entire body of knowledge in almost any way we can describe; possibly in ten years and probably within twenty, we shall be able to command machines to "mull over" separate subfields of the corpus and organize them for our use — if we can define precisely what "mulling" should mean and specify the kind of organization we require.

CHAPTER TWO

Aims, Requirements, Plans, and Criteria for Procognitive Systems

BROADLY SPEAKING, the aims of procognitive systems are to promote and facilitate the acquisition, organization, and use of knowledge. Let us examine these broad aims, and some of the general requirements associated with them, before moving on to more specific discussion of plans and criteria.

ACQUISITION OF KNOWLEDGE

The acquisition of knowledge — the initial apprehension of increments to the fund of knowledge — involves the recording and representation of events. It involves also a selective activity, directed from within the existing body of knowledge, and analyzing and organizing activities relating the increment to the existing body of knowledge.

Both the acquisitive and the interpretive aspects are recognized, and seen to play strongly interactive roles, in "experience" and in "experimentation." However, although the interpretive aspects are included within it, the acquisitive aspects are largely excluded from the present-day concept of library. That is to say, when a library acquires an increment to its holding, it acquires the increment from a publisher, not from "primary nature."

The segmentation of the over-all cognitive process appears to have arisen, not because it was thought to be inherently desirable to turn one's back on the fund of knowledge while seeking out new knowledge to augment it, but because there was no way to make, or let, the acquisition process interact more directly with the processes of organization and maintenance of the main body. In thinking about new systems that may not have to suffer from that lack, we should keep in mind the possibility of developing stronger interactions between the acquisition process and the processes that deal with the knowledge that already exists. The idea is illustrated schematically in Fig. 1.

To anchor the foregoing general consideration in a slightly more specific context, let us consider acquisition of knowledge through laboratory experimentation. The laboratory and the library are physically separate and distinct. The only channels for interaction between them are the telephone, the experimenter himself, and the books he borrows from the library and examines in the laboratory. The part of the fund of knowledge that interacts with nature *during* an experiment, therefore, is only that part that is stored inside the experimenter's head, plus small amounts that come into his head from books he reads or from calls he makes to the library while his experiment is running, or that are implicit in the design of his experimental apparatus. Only after he has collected

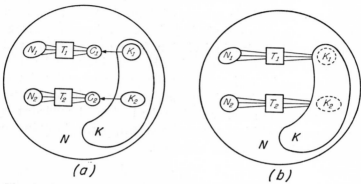

Fig. 1. (a) Schematic representation of the existing relation between acquisition of knowledge through experimentation and the library system. "Nature" is represented by N; the body of knowledge stored in the library, by K. A small part K_1 of K is understood in the form of some cognitive structure C_1 — that is located in the experimenter and his laboratory — by an experimenter who conducts an experiment T_1 upon a small part N_1 of N. The three lines connecting one figure with another represent an interaction constrained only by the nature of T_1. When the experimenter has collected and interpreted his data (not shown), he may write a paper that adds something to K_1.

(b) Illustrating the elimination of the constraints and limitations imposed by the interposition of the C_1 between the T_1 and the K of diagram a. The experiments may now interact with the whole of K, and particularly with all of K_1, using other channels of interaction in addition to those provided in diagram a (and now subsumed under the broader $T_1 - K$ interaction). The advantage of diagram b over diagram a depends, of course, upon the effectiveness of the added arrangements for interaction.

and analyzed his data does he go back to the library to investigate further their significance in relation to other parts of the body of knowledge. Thus the separation of

23

library from laboratory forces the use of "batching" procedures in the acquisition of knowledge and leads, at best, to the collection — in isolation from concurrent processes of acquisition, organization, and application — of large, monolithic masses of data. At worst, the data are collected, not only in isolation from these concurrent processes, but also in isolation from one another, and the result is a chaos of miscellaneous individual cases. The difficulties of integrating the results of many simultaneous research projects that operate with very loose linkage to one another and to the body of knowledge is at present the object of much concern, particularly in the field of pharmaceutical research.

ORGANIZATION OF KNOWLEDGE

We have referred repeatedly to "the fund of knowledge," "the body of knowledge," and "the corpus." The most concrete schemata that are useful in shaping the concepts associated with those terms are the schemata that represent the strings of alphanumeric characters, and the associated diagrams, graphs, pictures, and so forth, that make up the documents that are preserved in recognized repositories. However, such simple, concrete schemata are not in themselves sufficient. Neuroanatomy and neurophysiology, together with human behavior, provide less definite, but nevertheless necessary, supplementary schemata that enrich the concept. These complex arrangements of neuronal elements and processes accept diverse stimuli, including spoken and printed sentences, and somehow process and store them in ways that support the drawing of inferences and the answering of

24

questions; and though these responses are often imprecise, they are usually more appropriate to actual demands than mere reinstatement of past inputs could ever hope to be.

When we speak of organizing information into knowledge, we assume a set of concepts that involves many such schemata. The raw materials or inputs to the "organizer" are alphanumeric data, geometrical patterns, pictures, time functions, and the like. The outputs of the organized system are expressed in one or more of the input forms, but they are not mere reproductions or translations of particular inputs; they are suggestions, answers to questions, and made-to-order summaries of the kind that a good human assistant might prepare if he had a larger and more accurate memory and could process information faster. Concepts of the organizing process, and of the organization itself, are the objects of several of the studies that will be summarized in later pages.

In organizing knowledge, just as in acquiring knowledge, it would seem desirable to bring to bear upon the task the whole corpus, all at one time — or at any rate larger parts of it than fall within the bounds of any one man's understanding. This aim seems to call for direct interactions among various parts of the body of knowledge, and thus to support the requirement, suggested in the Introduction, for an active or directly processible store.

One part of the concept of organization, called "memory organization," deals with the design of memory structures and systems, as distinct from structures and systems of information or knowledge. Its aim is to achieve two resonances or congruences: (1) between the memory and the information patterns that are likely to be stored in it, and (2) between the memory and the requests (e.g., questions) that are likely to be directed to it.

USE OF KNOWLEDGE

Knowledge is used in directing the further advancement and organization of knowledge, in guiding the development of technology, and in carrying out most of the activities of the arts and the professions and of business, industry, and government. That is to say, the fund of knowledge finds almost continual and universal application. Its recursive applications have been mentioned under the headings, Acquisition of Knowledge and Organization of Knowledge. They require more direct lines of information flow than are now available, lines that may be controlled by, but do not flow exclusively through, human beings.

This same need seems even stronger and more evident in some of the nonrecursive uses — external applications — of knowledge, particularly in engineering. It should be possible, for example, to transfer an entire system of chemical formulas directly from the general fund of knowledge to a chemical process-control system, and to do so under human monitorship but not through human reading and key pressing. It should be possible for the logistics manager who wants to have in his "data base" the dimensions of the harbors of the world to connect his own information system, through a suitable retrieval filter, to the "Procognitive System of Congress." He should not have to assign a dozen employees to a week of searching, note taking, and card punching.

In general, as Fig. 2 suggests, it should be possible to

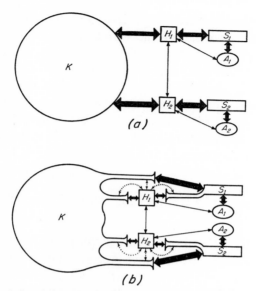

Fig. 2. (a) Simplified schematic representation illustrating the flow of information in present-day applications of the fund of knowledge K. Two applications, A_1 and A_2, are represented, each made by a human being H_1 working mainly through an application system S_1. The thickness of the lines represents the amount of information flow. All the information flows through the human beings.

(b) The situation that would prevail if, through the development of a procognitive system, the fund of knowledge were extended into intimate interactions (represented by the flared projections and their interfaces) with human users and their application systems. The dotted lines are control paths. Small amounts of control information are capable of directing the selection, transformation, and transmission of large amounts of substantive information. The human beings now function mainly as executives rather than mainly as relayers of information.

For complex applications involving several or many men, schema b should be extended, of course, to provide communication and coordination through S_1 and to let upper echelons exert control over lower-echelon channels.

27

transfer, directly from the general fund to the mechanism of a specific application, the various complexes or representations of knowledge required to support applications. The transfer should be requested and controlled through a process involving initial prescription, negotiated refinement of description, tests against various stated criteria, and human monitorship. To develop that general approach to application should be one of the main aims for procognitive systems.

PROCESSING VERSUS CONTROL AND MONITORING OF PROCESSING

In each of the three areas, acquisition, organization, and application, we are now greatly limited by the constraint that, whenever information flows into, within, or out of the main store of knowledge, it must pass through people. We shall not belabor the severity of the constraint. It is enough to note that a man, reading eight hours a day every work day, at a speed appropriate for novels, could just keep up with new "solid" contributions to a subfield of science or technology. It no longer seems likely that we can organize or distill or exploit the corpus by passing large parts of it through human brains. It is both our hypothesis and our conviction that people can handle the major part of their interaction with the fund of knowledge better by controlling and monitoring the processing of information than by handling all the detail directly themselves.

In order even to test the control-and-monitor approach, it is necessary first to externalize and make explicit the main procedures people employ — together with other procedures of equal or greater effectiveness — for dealing with stored information. It would doubtless be extremely difficult to accomplish that preliminary step if we included, among the main procedures, complete processes leading to insight and discovery. Eventually men may succeed in describing those "intelligent" processes completely and explicitly. If they do, we should like to incorporate the procedures into procognitive systems. However, the concept here under discussion does not depend upon complete programs for processes of such high sophistication. We are thinking in terms of lower-echelon procedures. The idea is merely to let people control the processing of the information in the body of knowledge by (1) applying named sequences or named hierarchal arrangements of procedures to named texts, graphs, and tables, (2) observing the results, and (3) intervening whenever a change or extension of plan is required.

We envision several different levels of abstraction in the control system and in its languages. At a procedure-oriented level, the system would be capable of implementing instructions such as the following:

1. Limit domain A in subsequent processing to *paragraphs* that contain at least *four words* of list x or their synonyms in *thesaurus y*.

2. Transform all the *sentences* of *document B* to kernel form.

3. Search domain C for instances of the form $u = v(w)$ or $w = v'(u)$ in which u and w are any names, v is any function name in *list z*, and v' appears in *list z* as the inverse of v.

4. If the information that meets the prescription can be displayed in *three pages*, display it now; otherwise display the number of *pages* required.

5. Select from domain *D* and add to *list t* each *sentence* that deals in any way with an *operation* upon something that contains, or can contain, something else that is mentioned in the *sentence*.

6. How many *documents* in the entire store have *sections* characterized by *g profiles* that correlate above *0.7* with the *g profile* of *section 3* of *document E*?

7. Change *0.7* in the foregoing to *0.8*. How many?

In the foregoing example of instructions in a hypothetical procedure-oriented language, each term in italics is to be regarded as a particular value of a variable; other terms of the suggested class would be equally admissible. Terms such as "limit . . . to," "domain," "subsequent," "processing," "contain," "at least," "of," "their," "or," "synonym," "in," and "transform," would have standard meanings within the system. There would be very many such terms. Only specialists would learn all the terms and their specific meanings. However, the language would offer some flexibility in the use of synonyms and much flexibility in selection of syntactic forms, and it would not take many months to become a specialist. Instruction 1, for example, could equally well be given as:

1*a*. Exclude henceforth from domain *A* all *paragraphs* not containing *four* or more *words* that are in *list x* or that are *thesaurus*-y synonyms of *words* that are in *list x*.

To devise and implement such a language — successful use of which demands substantive knowledge and clear thinking, but not rigid adherence to complex rules of format — will require an extrapolation, but an achievable extrapolation, of computer-programming languages.

With the aid of the language and procedures suggested in the preceding discussion, one could move onward to specialized languages, oriented toward particular fields or subfields of knowledge, that would be easier to learn and use. A servomechanisms engineer, for example, might employ a language in which instructions such as the following could be implemented:

1. Convert all the *Nyquist diagrams* in *set A* to *Bode plots.*

2. How many *reports* are there that contain *transfer functions* of *human operators* in nonlinear control systems?

3. How many of the *transfer functions* are for stochastic inputs?

4. Display the *transfer functions* one at a time on the *screen.*

5. Transfer W. E. Smith's AJAX simulation to my *Experiment C* data base as simulation *2.*

Obviously such a system must contain much substantive knowledge of its fields. A language for servo engineers will have to be developed in large part by servo engineers. Indeed, the only way to bring into being the many field-oriented languages required to support widespread use of procognitive systems will be (1) to attract leading members of the various substantive fields into pioneering work in the regions of overlap between the substantive fields and the information sciences, and (2) to provide them with ready-made component procedures, procedure-oriented languages designed to facilitate the development of field-oriented languages, and machines capable of putting the field-oriented languages to work and thus facilitating substantive research and application as soon as the languages are developed.

In any event, a basic part of the over-all aim for procognitive systems is to get the user of the fund of knowledge into something more nearly like an executive's or commander's position. He will still read and think and, hopefully, have insights and make discoveries, but he will not have to do all the searching himself nor all the transforming, nor all the testing for matching or compatibility that is involved in creative use of knowledge. He will say what operations he wants performed upon what parts of the body of knowledge, he will see whether the result makes sense, and then he will decide what to have done next. Some of his work will involve simultaneous interaction with colleagues and with the fund of stored knowledge. Nothing he does and nothing they do will impair the usefulness of the fund to others.* Hopefully, much that one user does in his interaction with the fund will make it more valuable to others.

Criteria for Procognitive Systems

The set of criteria that should or must be met in the design and development of procognitive systems includes economic elements and elements relating to technical feasibility as well as elements reflecting the needs and desires of potential users. It includes also some elements that will be governed mainly by quasi-philosophical attitudes toward courses to be followed and goals to be sought by man and civilization. Finally, it includes the consideration that there must be a way "to get there from here," whether the course be evolutionary (the expressed

---

* Except, of course, for the introduction of false information into the authenticated and organized core of the fund — but the procognitive system will be better protected than the present system is against the introduction of false information, because of its more elaborate editing, correlating, and organizing procedures.

preference of many present-day system technologists) or revolutionary.

Economic criteria tend to be dominant in our society. The economic value of information and knowledge is increasing. By the year 2000, information and knowledge may be as important as mobility. We are assuming that the average man of that year may make a capital investment in an "intermedium" or "console" — his intellectual Ford or Cadillac — comparable to the investment he makes now in an automobile, or that he will rent one from a public utility that handles information processing as Consolidated Edison handles electric power. In business, government, and education, the concept of "desk" may have changed from passive to active: a desk may be primarily a display-and-control station in a telecommunication-telecomputation system* — and its most vital part may be the cable ("umbilical cord") that connects it, via a wall socket, into the procognitive utility net. Thus our economic assumption is that interaction with information and knowledge will constitute 10 or 20 per cent of the total effort of the society, and the rational economic (or socioeconomic) criterion is that the society be more productive or more effective with procognitive systems than without.

Note that the allocation of resources to information systems in this projection covers interaction with bodies of information other than the body of knowledge now associated with libraries. The parts of the allocation that pay for user stations, for telecommunication, and for telecomputation can be charged in large part to the han-

* If a man wishes to get away from it all and think in peace and quiet, he will have merely to turn off the power. However, it may not be economically feasible for his employer to pay him at full rate for the time he thus spends in unamplified cerebration.

33

dling of everyday business, industrial, government, and professional information, and perhaps also to news, entertainment, and education. These more mundane activities will require extensive facilities, and parts of the neo-library procognitive system may ride on their coattails.

Whether or not, even with such help, the procognitive system can satisfy the economic criterion within our time scale depends heavily upon the future courses of our technology and our social philosophy. As indicated earlier, the technological prospect can be viewed only through uncertain speculation, but the prospect is fairly bright if the main trends of the information technology hold. The same cannot be said for the philosophical prospect because it is not as clear what the trends are.

To some extent, of course, the severity of the criteria that procognitive systems will be forced to meet will depend upon whether the pro- or anti-intellectual forces in our society prevail. It seems unlikely that widespread support for the development of procognitive systems will stem from appreciation of "the challenge to mankind," however powerful that appreciation may be in support of space efforts. The facts that information-processing systems lack the sex-symbolizing and attention-compelling attributes of rockets, that information is abstract whereas the planets and stars are concrete, and that procognitive systems may be misinterpreted as rivaling man instead of helping him — these facts may engender indifference or even hostility instead of support.

At the present time, in any event, not many people seem to be interested in intimate interaction with the fund of knowledge — but, of course, not many have any idea what such interaction would be like. Indeed, it would not be like anything in common experience. The only widespread schemata that are relevant at all are those derived from schooling, and they suffer from lack of relevance on precisely the critical point, intimacy of interaction. The few who do have somewhat appropriate schemata for projection of the picture — who have had the opportunity to interact intimately ("on line" in a good, flexible system) with a computer and its programs and data — are excited about the prospect and eager to move into the procognitive future, but they are indeed few. Even if their number should grow as rapidly as opportunity for on-line interaction will permit, they will constitute a cadre of useful specialists rather than a broad community of eager supporters.

The foregoing considerations suggest that the economic criterion will be rigidly enforced, that procognitive systems will have to prove their value in dollars before they will find widespread demand. If so, procognitive systems will come into being gradually, first in the richest, densest areas of application, which will be found mainly in government and business, and only later in areas in which the store of information is poor or dilute. Close interaction with the general fund of knowledge, which is on the whole neither rich nor dense, will be deferred, if these assumptions are correct, until developments paid for by special procognitive applications have made the broader effort practicable. Such a "coattail" ride on a piecemeal carrier may not be the best approach for the nation or the society as a whole, but it seems to be the most probable one. In any event, it is beyond the present scope to determine an optimal course through the quasi-philosophical and socioeconomic waters.

The criteria that are clearly within our scope are those that pertain to the needs and desires of users. The main criteria in that group appear to be that the procognitive system:

1. Be available when and where needed.
2. Handle both documents and facts.*
3. Permit several different categories of input, ranging from authority-approved formal contributions (e.g., papers accepted by recognized journals) to informal notes and comments.
4. Make available a body of knowledge that is organized both broadly and deeply — and foster the improvement of such organization through use.
5. Facilitate its own further development by providing tool-building languages and techniques to users and preserving the tools they devise and by recording measures of its own performance and adapting in such a way as to maximize the measures.
6. Provide access to the body of knowledge through convenient procedure-oriented and field-oriented languages.
7. Converse or negotiate with the user while he formulates his requests and while responding to them.
8. Adjust itself to the level of sophistication of the individual user, providing terse, streamlined modes for experienced users working in their fields of expertness, and functioning as a teaching machine to guide and improve the efforts of neophytes.
9. Permit users to deal either with metainformation (through which they can work "at arms length" with

* "Facts," used here in a broad sense, refers to items of information or knowledge derived from one or more documents and not constrained to the form or forms of the source passages. It refers also to items of information or knowledge in systems or subsystems that do not admit subdivision into documentlike units.

36

substantive information), or with substantive information (directly), or with both at once.

10. Provide the flexibility, legibility, and convenience
of the printed page at input and output and, at the same
time, the dynamic quality and immediate responsiveness
of the oscilloscope screen and light pen.

11. Facilitate joint contribution to and use of knowledge by several or many co-workers.

12. Present flexible, wide-band interfaces to other systems, such as research systems in laboratories, informa-
tion-acquisition systems in government, and application
systems in business and industry.

13. Reduce markedly the difficulties now caused by
the diversity of publication languages, terminologies, and
"symbologies."

14. Essentially eliminate publication lag.

15. Tend toward consolidation and purification of
knowledge instead of, or as well as, toward progressive
growth and unresolved equivocation.*

16. Evidence neither the ponderousness now associated with overcentralization nor the confusing diversity
and provinciality now associated with highly distributed
systems. (The user is presumably indifferent to the design decisions through which this is accomplished.)

17. Display desired degree of initiative, together with
good selectivity, in dissemination of recently acquired and
"newly needed" knowledge.

To the foregoing criteria, it may be fair to add criteria
that are now appreciated more directly by librarians
than by the users of libraries. Some of the following cri-

---

* It may be desirable to preserve, in a secondary or tertiary store,
many contributions that do not qualify as "solid" material for the
highly organized, rapidly accessible nucleus of the body of knowledge.

teria are, as they should be, largely implicit in the fore-going list, but it will do no harm to make them explicit.

18. Systematize and expedite the cataloguing and indexing* of new acquisitions, forcing conformity to the system's cataloguing standards at the time of "publication" and distributing throughout the system the fruits of all labor devoted to indexing and other aspects of organization.

19. Solve the problem of (mainly by eliminating) recovery of documents.

20. Keep track of users' interests and needs and implement acquisition and retention policy (policy governing what to hold in local memories) for each local subsystem.

21. Record all chargeable uses, and handle bookkeeping and billing. Also record all charges that the system itself incurs, and handle their bookkeeping and payment.

22. Provide special facilities (languages, processors, displays) for use by system specialists and by teams made up of system and substantive specialists in their continual efforts to improve the organization of the fund of knowledge. (This professional, system-oriented work on organization is supplemented by the contributions toward organization made by ordinary users in the course of their substantive interaction with the body of knowledge.)

23. Provide special administrative and judicial facilities (again languages, processors, displays) for use in arriving at and implementing decisions that affect over-all system policies and rules.

The list of criteria ends with two considerations that

---

* "Indexing" is subsumed under "organization" in our use of the latter term in connection with documents or corpora.

we think many users will deem extremely important in a decade or two, but few would mention now:

24. Handle formal procedures (computer programs, subroutines, and so forth, written in formal, machine-independent languages) as well as the conventional documents and facts mentioned in criterion 2.

25. Handle heuristics (guidelines, strategies, tactics, and rules of thumb intended to expedite solution of problems) coded in such a way as to facilitate their association with situations to which they are germane.

The foregoing criteria are set forth, we recognize, essentially as absolute desiderata, and not — as system criteria should be — as scales of measurement with relative weights, interdependent cutoff points, or other paraphernalia for use in optimization. The reason for stopping so far short of an explicit decision procedure is partly that it is very difficult to set up such a procedure for so complex a system, but mainly that it is too early to foresee the details of interaction among the decision factors. The foregoing lists are intended not to provide a complete mechanism for the evaluation of plans, but merely to invite discussion and emendation and to furnish a context for examination of the "plan" that follows.

PLAN FOR A SYSTEM TO MEDIATE INTERACTIONS WITH THE FUND OF KNOWLEDGE

The plan to be presented here is not a plan to be implemented by a single organization. It is not a system design or a management plan. Rather, it is a rough outline of researches and developments, many of which will probably be carried out, plan or no plan, during the next

39

several decades. The reason for setting forth such a plan is not to guide research and development, which would be presumptuous, but to provide a kind of checklist or scorecard for use in following the game. If the technology should take care of most of the items in the plan but fall behind on a few, then it might be worth while for an agency interested in the outcome to foster special efforts on the delinquent items.

Moreover, this plan is not a final plan or even a mature plan. Perhaps it should be regarded only as a set of suggestions, made by a small group without expertness in all the potentially contributory disciplines, toward the formulation of a plan for a system to facilitate man's interaction with the store of knowledge. For the sake of brevity, however, let us call it a plan. It will be convenient to discuss it in two parts:

1. The structure and functions of the proposed system.

2. Approaches to realization of the proposed system through research, technology development, and system development.

Structure and functions of proposed system

The proposed procognitive system has a hierarchical structure of the kind mentioned earlier: system, subsystem, . . . component. It seems at first glance to be hierarchical also in another way: it has a top-echelon or central subsystem, several second-echelon or regional subsystems, many third-echelon or local subsystems, and very many fourth-echelon subsystems or user stations. Actually, however, as Fig. 3 illustrates, there are departures from the simple, treelike paradigm of a true hierarchy. First, for the sake of reliability and what the military calls "survivability," the top-echelon subsystem should be replicated. However, it may not be possible, or

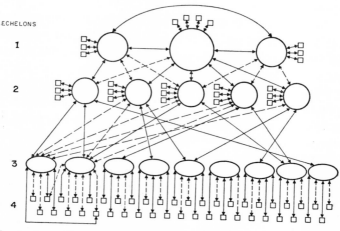

Fig. 3. Over-all structure of the procognitive system. The circles and ellipses represent advanced and specialized computer systems. The squares represent man-computer interfaces, those of echelon 4 being stations or consoles for substantive users of the system. Most of the connections are switchable telecommunication links. Those shown as solid lines represent connections that might be established at a particular moment during operation. The dotted lines are introduced to suggest other connections that could be established.

The centers of echelon 1 are concerned primarily with maintaining the total fund of knowledge, those of echelon 2 with organizing the corpora of fields or subfields of knowledge, and those of echelon 3 with the processing required by users in various localities. The user stations of echelon 4 provide input and output (control and display) facilities and perhaps some processing and memory associated with control and display.

Except in echelon 1, the number of subsystems envisioned for the projected system is very much greater than the number shown.

even desirable, to give the replicates all the capabilities of the main subsystem. Second, each third-level subsystem may be connected to any higher-level subsystem, and to more than one higher-level subsystem at a time. Technically speaking, that makes the structure a lattice instead of a hierarchy. Perhaps it will be best to call it simply a "network."

The best schema available for thinking about the third and fourth echelons is provided by the multiple-console time-sharing computer systems recently developed, or under development, at Massachusetts Institute of Technology, Cargenie Institute of Technology, System Development Corporation, RAND Corporation, Bolt Beranek and Newman, and a few other places. In order to provide a good model, it is necessary to borrow features from the various time-sharing systems and assemble them into a composite schema. Note that the fourth-echelon subsystems are user stations and that the third-echelon subsystems are intended primarily to provide short-term storage and processing capability to local users, not to serve as long-term repositories.

The second-echelon subsystems are structurally more like computer systems than libraries or documentation centers, though they function more like libraries. A typical second-echelon subsystem is essentially a digital computer* with many processors, memory blocks, and input-output units working in parallel and with a large and advanced memory hierarchy, plus a sophisticated digital

---

* It is possible that, before operationally significant procognitive systems are developed, another kind of information processor will displace, from its prime position in information technology, what we now recognize as the digital computer. It seems to us unlikely that devices of the perceptron type will best fulfill the purposes with which we are here concerned, but other schemata exist and still more are conceivable, and plenty of time remains for us to be openminded. In any event, the design of digital computers is departing from the Princeton paradigm, and the next decade may see as much diversity of structure among digital computers as the last decade saw homogeneity.

communication terminal and stations for use by its own specialists in operating and in organizing. Each second-echelon subsystem handles one or more than one substantive field or subfield * of knowledge. Two or three subsystems may work partly in parallel and partly in complement in the largest and most active fields or subfields.

The top-echelon subsystems are similar in general schema to the second-echelon subsystems. The top echelon is specialized (1) to preserve the body of knowledge, (2) to add to it progressively the distilled contributions received from second-echelon subsystems, (3) to transfer information to lower-echelon subsystems on request, and (4) to improve the organization of the over-all fund in ways complementary to those pursued in the second-echelon subsystems.

The top-echelon memory is, therefore, extremely large. Its design may have to sacrifice speed to achieve the necessary size. For several decades, indeed, it seems likely that the limitations on memory size will completely dominate the picture, and that there will be little hope of achieving a strongly interpenetrating organization of the over-all body of knowledge. In the interim, the top echelon will be limited essentially to the first three functions.

Until the top echelon can take up function (4) effectively, it may be desirable to "organize around the problem" in the following way: Use the top echelon, in the manner described, to fulfill the first three functions. Create several special second-echelon subsystems to deal with cross-field interactions, limiting them to fields (or subfields) that are judged likely to have important overlaps or significant interconnections. These special second-

---

* At first, it will be possible only to handle subfields. As technology advances, it may become possible to bring related subfields together and to handle an entire field of knowledge in a single subsystem.

echelon subsystems may not be able to operate on the entire corpora of the fields or subfields with which they are concerned; they may have to use highly distilled representations. Even with such limitations, however, they should be able to make valuable contributions by fostering homogeneity of practice from field to field, detecting apparent duplications and complementations in related fields, and noting similarities of form or structure in models or other information structures employed in substantively diverse areas.

The number of centers in echelon 1 envisioned for a national * system is approximately three, as shown in Fig. 3. In echelon 2, the number of centers should correspond roughly to the number of fields (approximately 100) or subfields (approximately 1000) into which knowledge is subdivided for deep analysis and organization. In echelon 3, the number of centers should correspond to the number of localities in which significant interaction with the body of knowledge occurs. "Localities" will be large areas if the economic advantage of large information-processing systems over small ones tends to outweigh the incremental cost (associated with the greater distances in larger areas) of communication between user stations and centers; they will be small if communication costs tend to dominate. Large organizations may maintain their own third-echelon centers and use them in processing proprietary information as well as information from or for the general fund. And the number of third-echelon centers will, of course, depend upon the demand. These considerations make projection of

* This discussion is focused on a system appropriate for the United States or perhaps for North America. The ways in which the structure of a world-wide system would differ depend critically on the future economics of intercontinental telecommunication.

44

the number of third-echelon centers highly uncertain. It falls somewhere between 20 and 2000. We have already examined some aspects of the fourth-echelon user stations. There will be hundreds of thousands of user stations, though many of them will be used only intermittently.

Ordinarily, a user will dial his own nearby third-echelon center and use its processing and memory facilities. His center will probably be holding some of his personal data or procedures in its store, and, in addition, using the local center will keep down the transmission costs. However, when a user wishes to work with a distant colleague, and to pool his personal data with those of his colleague, he can dial the remote center and request transmission of his data to it.*

A hypothetical example of use of the procognitive system

Perhaps the best way to consolidate the picture that we have been projecting, one part at a time, is to describe a series of interactions, between the system and a user who is working on a substantive problem that requires access to, and manipulation of, the fund of knowledge. Let us choose an example that will exercise the system in several ways — and try to compensate for the complexity thus necessarily introduced by describing the interaction in detail only in the first episode, and then moving to a higher level of abstraction. Let us, for the sake of brevity, refer to the system as "system" and to the user as "I." And, finally, let us use in the example a fairly straightforward descriptor-based approach to document

---

* Other arrangements for cooperative work may prove superior to the one suggested. Our purpose here is merely to note that the need will exist and can be met.

retrieval, even though that facet of the art should be greatly advanced by 1994, and even though we shall not hesitate in the same example to assume a question-answering capability that is much farther advanced than the document-retrieval capability.

Friday afternoon — I am becoming interested, let us say, in the prospect that digital computers can be programmed in such a way as to "understand" passages of natural language. (That is a 1964 problem, but let us imagine that I have available in 1964 the procognitive system of 1994.) In preparation for a session of study on Monday, I sit down at my console to place an advance order for study materials. I take this foresighted approach because I am not confident that the subject matter has been organized well in the store of the procognitive system, or even that the material I wish to examine is all in one subfield center.

Immediately before me on my console is a typewriter that is, in its essentials, quite like a 1964 office typewriter except that there is no direct connection between the keyboard and the marking unit. When I press a key, a code goes into the system, and the system then sends back a code (which may or may not be the one I sent), and the system's code activates the marking unit. To the right of typewriter, and so disposed that I can get into position to write on it comfortably if I rotate my chair a bit, is an input-output screen, a flat surface 11" × 14" on which the system and I can print, write, and draw to each other. It is easy to move this surface to a position above the typewriter for easy viewing while I type, but, because I like to write and draw my inputs to the system, I usually leave the screen in its horizontal position beside the type-

46

writer. In a penholder beside the screen is a pen that can mark on the screen very much as an ordinary pen marks on paper, except that there is an "erase" mode. The co-ordinates of each point of each line marked on the screen are sensed by the system. The system then "recognizes" and interprets the marks. Inside the console is a camera-projector focused upon the screen. Above the chair is a microphone. The system has a fair ability to recognize speech sounds, and it has a working vocabulary that con-tains many convenient control words. Unfortunately, however, my microphone is out of order. There is a power switch, a microphone switch, a camera button, and a pro-jector button. That is all. The console is not one of the high-status models with several viewing screens, a page printer, and spoken output.

The power is on, but I have not yet been in interaction with the system. I therefore press a typewriter key — any key — to let the system know the station is going into operation. The system types back, and simultaneously displays upon the screen:

14:23 13 November 1964

Are you J. C. R. Licklider?

(The system knows that I am the most frequent, but not the only, user of this console.) I type "y" for yes, and the system, to provide a neat record on the right-hand side of the page, types:

J. C. R. Licklider

and makes a carriage return. (When the system types, the typewriter operates very rapidly; it typed my name in a fifth of a second.) The display on the screen has now lost the "Are you . . ." and shows only the date and name. Incidentally, the typing that originates with me always appears in red; what originates in the computer always appears in black.

At this early stage of the proceedings, I am interacting with the local center, but the local center is also a subsystem of systems other than the procognitive system. Since I wish to use the procognitive system, I type

```
Procog
```

and receive the reply:

You are now in the Procognitive System.

To open the negotiation, I ask the procognitive system:

```
What are your descriptor expressions for:
    computer processing of natural language
    computer processing of English
    natural-language control of computers
    natural-language programming of
        computers
DIGRESS
```

At the point at which I wrote "DIGRESS," it occurred to me that I might in a short while be using some of the phrases repeatedly, and that it would be convenient to define temporary abbreviations. The typed strings were appearing on the display screen as well as the paper. (I usually leave the console in the mode in which the information, when it will fit and not cause delay, is presented on both the typewriter and the screen.) I therefore type:

```
define temp
```

On recognizing the phrase, which is a frequently used control phrase, the system locks my keyboard and takes the initiative with:

48

define temporarily

via typewriter? via screen?

I answer by swiveling to the screen, picking up the pen, and pointing to **screen** on the screen. I then point to the beginning and end of **computer processing**, then to the **c** and the **p,** and then to a little square on the screen labeled "end symbol." (Several such squares, intended to facilitate control by pointing, appear on the screen in each mode.)

In making the series of designations by pointing just described, I took advantage of my knowledge of a convenient format that is available in the mode now active. The first two pointings designate the beginning and end of the term to be defined, and the next pointings, up to "end symbol," spell out the abbreviation. (Other formats are available in the current mode, and still others in other modes.) If my microphone had been working, I should have said "Define *cee pee* abbreviation *this*" and drawn a line across **computer processing** as I said *"this."* The system would then have displayed on the screen its interpretation of the instruction, and then (after waiting a moment for me to intervene) implemented it.

Next, I define abbreviations for "natural language" (nl), "computer" (comp), and "programming" (prog). (Unless instructed otherwise, the system uses the same abbreviation for singular and plural forms and for hyphenated and unhyphenated forms.) And finally, insofar as this digression is concerned, I touch a small square on the screen labeled "end digression," return to the typewriter, and type:

```
comp understanding of nl
comp comprehension of semantic relations?§
```

49

The question mark terminates the query, and the symbol § tells the system not to wait for further input from me now.

Because the system's over-all thesaurus is very large, and since I did not specify any particular field or subfield of knowledge, I have to wait while the requested information is derived from tertiary memory. That takes about 10 seconds. In the interim, the system suggests that I indicate what I want left on the display screen. I draw a closed line around the date, my name, and the query. The line and everything outside it disappear. Shortly thereafter, the system tells me:

Response too extensive to fit on screen. Do you wish short version, multipage display, or typewriter-only display?

Being in a better position to type than to point, I type:

s

That is enough to identify my preference. The short version appears on the screen but not the typewriter — I rather expected it there too):

Descriptor expressions:
1. (natural language) ∧ (computer processing of)
2. (natural language) ∧ (on-line man-computer interaction)
3. (natural language) ∧ (machine translation of)
4. (natural language) ∧ (computer programming)
5. (computer program) ∧ (semantic net)
6. (compiler) ∧ (semantic)
Descriptor inclusions:
7. (natural language) includes (English)
Phrase equivalences:

50

8. (control of computers) ≃ (on-line man-machine interaction)
9. (programming of computers) ≃ (computer programming)
10. (semantic relations) ≃ (semantic nets)

[END]

I am happy with 1 and especially happy with 2. I am curious about 5. I think I should look into 4. Number 3 frightens me a little, because I suspect it will lead to too much semirelevant information. I think I recognize 6 as a false lead into the field of program compiling, in which field, although "syntax" seems to be used in essentially the linguist's sense, "semantics" is used in what appears to me to be an inscrutable kind of jargon. Accordingly, I type to the system:

```
Prepare bibliographies with abstracts
   (1, 2, 4, 5).
Best 25 references each.  When will they
   be available?
```

Before turning control over to the system, I decide to ask a substantive question, even though I realize I do not yet know enough about the subject to inquire intelligently. Using the control word, "QUESTION," to establish the mode, I ask:

```
QUESTION:  Has any digital-computer system
responded to questions phrased in ordinary
English, or other natural language, by
giving correct answers in natural
language? §
```

The system replies first to "When will they be available?"

51

Requested bibliographies will be available at about 18:00.
Do you want them delivered, or will you call, or will you request typeout?

Unfortunately, my office is not located near a pneumatic-tube station. I rely heavily on typeouts made by the system when I am away from the console. I reply:

```
Type them out as soon as they are
   available.
```

The system reminds me:

Please leave your console power on!

Then it replies to the "QUESTION":

Cannot give yes-no answer to QUESTION. Approaches to "yes" are described in the following:

1. B. F. Green, A. K. Wolf, C. Chomsky, and K. Laughery, Baseball: An Automatic Question-Answerer, Proc. Western Joint Computer Conf., 19, 219–224, 1961.

2. S. Klein and R. F. Simmons, A Computational Approach to Grammatical Coding of English Words, J. Assoc. Computing Machinery, 10, 334–347, 1963.

3. S. Klein and R. F. Simmons, Syntactic Dependence and the Computer Generation of Coherent Discourse, Mechanical Translation (entering system).

The foregoing must suffice to suggest the nature of the interaction at the level of key pressing and pointing. The console hardware and procedure embody many features, worked out through the years, that maximize convenience and free the user from clerical routine. The formats and procedures are quite flexible. The user learns, through working with the system, what modes and techniques suit him best. Ordinarily, he gives the system rather terse, almost minimal instructions, relying on it to interpret them correctly and to do what he wishes and expects.

When it misinterprets him or gets off the track of his thinking, as it sometimes does, he falls back on more explicit expression of commands and queries.

To continue with our example, let us move on to Monday. The reference citations and abstracts are ready for examination. The system has anticipated that I may want to see or process the full texts, and they are now available in secondary memory, having been moved up from the tertiary store along with a lot of other, somewhat less clearly relevant, material. I do not know exactly how much of such anticipatory preparation has gone on within the system, but I know that the pressure of on-line requests is low during the week-end, and I am counting on the system to have done a fair amount of work on my behalf. (I could have explicitly requested preparatory assembly and organization of relevant material, but it is much less expensive to let the system take the initiative. The system tends to give me a fairly high priority because I often contribute inputs intended to improve its capabilities.) Actually, the system has been somewhat behind schedule in its organization of information in the field of my interest, but over the week-end it retrieved over 10,000 documents, scanned them all for sections rich in relevant material, analyzed all the rich sections into statements in a high-order predicate calculus, and entered the statements into the data base of the question-answering subsystem.

It may be worthwhile to digress here to suggest how the system approached the problem of selecting relevant documents. The approach to be described is not advanced far beyond the actual state of the art in 1964. Certainly, a more sophisticated approach will be feasible before 1994.

All contributions to the system are assigned tentative descriptors when the contributions are generated. The system maintains an elaborate thesaurus of descriptors and related terms and expressions. The thesaurus recognizes many different kinds of relations between and among terms. It recognizes different meanings of a given term. It recognizes logical categories and syntactic categories. The system spends much time maintaining and improving this thesaurus. As soon as it gets a chance, it makes statistical analyses of the text of a new acquisition and checks the tentatively assigned descriptors against the analyses. It also makes a combined syntactic-semantic analysis of the text, and reduces every sentence to a (linguistic) canonical form and also to a set of expressions in a (logical) predicate calculus. If it has serious difficulty in doing any of these things, it communicates with the author or editor, asking help in solving its problem or requesting revision of the text. It tests each unexpectedly frequent term (word or unitary phrase) of the text against grammatical and logical criteria to determine its appropriateness for use as a descriptive term, draws up a set of working descriptors and subdescriptors, sets them into a descriptor structure, and, if necessary, updates the general thesaurus.*

In selecting documents that may be relevant to a retrieval prescription, the system first sets up a descriptor structure for the prescription. This structure includes all the terms of the prescription that are descriptors or subdescriptors at any level in the thesaurus. It includes, also, thesaurus descriptors and subdescriptors that are synonymous to, or related in any other definite way to, terms

---

* New entries into the general thesaurus are dated. They remain tentative until proven through use.

54

of the prescription that are not descriptors or subdescriptors in the thesaurus. All the logical relations and modulations of the prescription are represented in its descriptor structure.

The descriptor structure of a document is comparable to the descriptor structure of a prescription. The main task of the system in screening documents for relevance, therefore, is to measure the degrees of correlation or congruence that exist between various parts of the prescription's structure and corresponding parts, if they exist, of each document's structure. This is done by an algorithm (the object of intensive study during development of the system) that determines how much various parts of one structure have to be distorted to make them coincide with parts of another. The algorithm yields two basic measures for each significant coincidence: (1) degree of match, and (2) size of matching substructure. The system then goes back to determine, for each significant coincidence, (3) the amount of text associated with the matching descriptor structure. All three measures are available to the user. Ordinarily, however, he works with a single index, which he is free to define in terms of the three measures. When the user says "best references," the system selects on the basis of his index. If the user has not defined an index, of course, the system defines one for him, knowing his fields of interest, who his colleagues are, how they defined their indexes, and so forth.

We shall not continue this digression to examine the question-answering or other related facilities of the system. Discussions relevant to them are contained in Part II. Let us return now to the conclusion of the example.

I scan the lists of references and read the abstracts. I begin to get some ideas about the structure of the field, and to appreciate that it is in a fairly primitive stage. Evidently, it is being explored mainly by linguists, logicians, psychologists, and computer scientists, and they do not speak a uniform language. My interest is caught most strongly by developments in mathematical syntax. The bibliography contains references to work by Noam Chomsky, Ida Rhodes, A. G. Oettinger, V. E. Giuliano, V. H. Yngve, and others. I see that I was wrong in neglecting machine translation. I correct that error right away. The requested bibliography appears at once; the system had discovered the relevance and was prepared.

The first thing I wish to clear up is whether the syntactic and semantic parts of language are, or should be, handled separately or in combination in computer analysis of text. I give the system a series of questions and commands that includes:

```
Refer to bibliographies I requested last
Friday.
Do cited or related references contain
explicit definitions of "syntax",
"syntactics", or "semantic"?
Do syntactic analyses of sentences yield
many alternative parsings?
Give examples showing alternatives.  Give
examples illustrating how many.
Is there a description of a procedure in
which an analysis based on mathematical
syntax is used in tandem or in alternation
with semantic analysis?
Display the description.
How long is Oettinger's syntactic
analyzer?
Do you have it available now? §
```

It turns out that Oettinger, Kuno and their colleagues have developed a series of syntactic analyzers and that the most recent one has been documented and introduced into the procognitive system (Oettinger and Kuno, 1962). I do not have to bother Oettinger himself — at least not yet.

I request that the program be retrieved and prepared for execution by asking:

```
What arguments and control operations does
the routine require?  What formats?  How
do I test it?
How do I apply the routine to a test
sentence?
```

The system tells me that all I have to do to apply the routine to a short test sentence, now that the system has the routine all ready to go, is to type the sentence; but for long inputs there are rules that I can ask to see. I type a sentence discussed by Kuno and Oettinger (1963):

```
They are flying planes.
```

The result pours forth on the screen in the form of a table full of abbreviations. I think I can probably figure out what the abbreviations mean, but it irritates me when the system uses unexplained abbreviations in a field that I am just beginning to study. I ask the system to associate the spelled-out terms with the abbreviations in the table. It does so, in very fine print, and appends a note citing the program write-up that explains the notations. I can barely make out the fine print. Partly to make sure of my reading, and partly to exercise the system (which still has a certain amount of plaything appeal), I touch "1V" on the tree diagram with the stylus, and then hold the stylus a moment on the control spot labeled "magnify." The tree expands around the "1V," enlarging the print, and thereby lets me confirm my uncertain reading of "level one, predicative verb."

My next step is to test a sentence of my own. After

that, I ask to see the other programs in the system that are most closely similar in function to the one just examined. The system gives me first a list of the names and abstracts of several syntax programs, and then as I call for them, the write-ups and listings, and it makes each program available for testing. I explore the programs, but not yet very deeply. I wish merely to gain an impression from direct interaction with them and then go back to a mixture of reading and asking questions of the system.

The foregoing is doubtless enough to suggest the nature of the interaction with the fund of knowledge that we think would be desirable. None of the functions involved in the interaction described in the example is very complex or profound. Almost surely the functions can be implemented in software* sooner than the hardware required to support them will be available. As the example suggests, we believe that useful information-processing services can be made available to men without the programming of computers to "think" on their own. We believe that much can be accomplished, indeed, without demanding many fundamental insights on the part of the initial designers of the system.

Perhaps we did not rely heavily enough, in the example and in the study, on truly sophisticated contributions from the inanimate components of the system. In respect of that possibility, we adopted a deliberately and admittedly conservative attitude. We expect that computers will be capable of making quite "intelligent" contributions by 1994, to take the date assumed in the example, but we prefer not to count on it. If valuable contributions can

---

* Computer programs, descriptions of procedure, dictionaries, instructional material, and so forth, as opposed to hardware, which is usually taken to include the processors, memories, display devices, communication equipment, and other such components of the system.

be made by "artificial intelligences" of that date, there will be room for them, as well as the men to monitor them, in our basic system schema. On the other hand, if it should turn out that the problems involved in developing significant artificial intelligence are extremely difficult, or that society rejects the whole idea of artificial intelligence as a defiance of God or a threat to man, then it will be good not to have counted on much help from software approaches that are not yet well enough understood to support extrapolation. This conservative attitude seems appropriate for the software area but not for the hardware area.

Steps toward Realization of Procognitive Systems

Our information technology is not yet capable of constructing a significant, practical system of the type we have been discussing. If it were generally agreed, as we think it should be, that such a system is worth striving for, then it would be desirable to have an implementation program. The first part of such a program should not concern itself directly with system development. It should foster advancement of relevant sectors of technology.*

Let us assume then — though without insisting — that it is in the interest of society to accelerate the advances. What particular things should be done?

Overcome interdisciplinary barriers

One of the first things to do, according to our study, is to break down the barriers that separate the potentially

---

* Science is also involved, of course, but for the sake of brevity "technology" is used in a very broad sense in this part of the discussion.

contributory disciplines. Among the disciplines relevant to the development of procognitive systems are (1) the library sciences, including the part of information storage and retrieval associated with the field of documentation, (2) the computer sciences, including both hardware and software aspects and the part of information storage and retrieval associated with computing, (3) the system sciences, which deal with the whole spectrum of problems involved in the design and development of systems, and (4) the behavioral and social sciences, parts of which are somewhat (and should be more) concerned with how people obtain and use information and knowledge. (The foregoing is not, of course, an exhaustive list; it even omits mathematical linguistics and mathematical logic, both of which are fundamental to the analysis and transformation of recorded knowledge.) The barriers that separate the relevant disciplines appear to be strong. There is, of course, some multidisciplinary work, and a little of it is excellent. On the whole, however, the potentially contributory disciplines are not effectively conjoined. One of the most necessary steps toward realization of procognitive systems is to promote positive interaction among them.

Develop the concept of relevance network

A second fundamental step is to determine basic characteristics of the relevance network that interrelates the elements of the fund of knowledge. The information elements of a sentence are interrelated by syntactic structures and semantic links. The main syntactic structures are obviously local; they scarcely span the spaces between sentences. Correspondence between syntactic structures is of some help in determining the type and degree of relation between two widely separated segments of text, but the main clues to the relations that interconnect diverse parts of the corpus of recorded information are semantic.

There is, therefore, a need for an effective, formal, analytical semantics. With such a tool, one might hope to construct a network in which every element of the fund of knowledge is connected to every other element to which it is significantly related. Each link might be thought of as carrying a code identifying the nature of the relation. The nature might be analyzed into type and degree.* Multiple-argument relations would be represented by multiple linkages. We use the term, "relevance network," to stand for this entire concept.

The magnitude of the task of organizing the corpus of recorded information into a coherent body of knowledge depends critically upon the average length of the links of the relevance network. To develop this idea, let us visualize the network as a reticulation of linkages connecting information elements in documents that are arranged spatially in a pattern corresponding to some classification system such as the Dewey Decimal. Now let us determine, for each element i, the number N_{ij} of links of each degree j that connect it to other elements, and determine, at the same time, the total length L_{ij} of all its links of each degree j. The average length of all the links of degree j in the network is

$$L_j = (\sum_i L_{ij}) / (\sum_i N_{ij})$$

If we weight the lengths by an inverse function such as

---

* Here "degree" implies a formalization of the intuitive notion that some relations are direct and immediate (e.g., x is the mother of y) whereas others are indirect and mediate (e.g., x is a member of a club of the same type as a club of which y is a member). Low degree corresponds to direct and immediate.

61

$1/j^2$ of their degrees, we have as an index for the average weighted length of the links:

$$L = \underset{j}{\Sigma} L_j / j^2$$

In order to determine the foregoing quantities precisely, one would have to carry out much of the task of organizing the body of knowledge, but we are concerned here mainly with the abstract concept, and sampling experiments would, in any event, suffice to make it concrete.

If at the outset we could fit the entire corpus into a giant random-access memory, we should not be concerned with the lengths of links. The total number of elements and the total number of links up to some cutoff degree would provide the bases for estimating the magnitude of the task of organizing the body of knowledge. However, as long as we can fit into processible memory only one part of the corpus at a time, it will be critical whether the linked elements of the relevance network cluster, and whether the memory will accept a typical cluster. The index L bears on that question. If L turns out to be small, then knowledge does indeed tend to cluster strongly, and part-by-part processing of the corpus will be effective. If L turns out to be large, then far-flung associations are prevalent, and we must await the development of a large memory.

In the foregoing discussion, the index L was based upon "lengths" in a space defined to correspond with a linear classification scheme. Obviously, that assumption, and many other parts of the suggested picture, need to be sharpened. One should not adopt the first paradigm to come to mind, but should explore the implications of various alternative properties and metrics of the relevance space. Moreover, one should regard the lengths of links and the metrics of the space merely as preliminary working conveniences, for all the lengths within a part of the corpus become equal when that part is loaded into a random-access memory, and the distance of that part from the other parts may, for practical purposes, become infinite. It is of paramount importance not to think of relevance as a vague, unanalyzed relation, but rather to try to distinguish among definite types and degrees of relevance. With such development, the concept of relevance networks might progress from its present unelaborated form to a systematic, analytic paradigm for organization of the body of knowledge.

Develop advanced memory systems

The most necessary hardware development appears to be in the area of memory, which we have already discussed. Procognitive systems will pose requirements for very large memories and for advanced memory organizations. Unless an unexpected breakthrough reconciles fast random access with very large capacity, there will be a need for memories that effect various compromises between those desiderata. They will comprise the echelons of the memory hierarchy we have mentioned. It will be necessary to develop techniques for transferring information on demand, and in anticipation of demand, from the slow, more voluminous levels of the hierarchy to the faster, more readily processible levels.

Insofar as memory media are concerned, current research and development present many possibilities. The most immediate prospects advanced for primary memories are thin magnetic films, coated wires, and cryogenic films. For the next echelons, there are magnetic disks and photographic films and plates. Farther distant are thermoplastics and photosensitive crystals. Still farther away — almost wholly speculative — are protein molecules and other quasi-living structures. All these possibilities will be explored by industry without special prodding, but it may in some instances be difficult for industry, unassisted, to move from demonstrations of feasibility in the laboratory into efficient production.

Associative, or content-addressable, memories are beginning to make their appearance in the computer technology. The first generation is, of course, too small and too expensive for applications of the kind we are interested in here, but the basic schema seems highly relevant. One version of the schema has three kinds of registers: a mask register, a comparison register, and many memory registers. All the registers have the same capacity except that each memory register has a special marker cell not found in the mask and comparison registers. The contents of the mask register are set to designate the part of the comparison and memory registers upon which attention is to be focused. The comparison and memory registers contain patterns. Suppose that "golf" falls within the part of the comparison register designated as active by the mask. When the "compare" instruction is given, the marker is set to 1 in the marker cell of every memory register that contains "golf" in the part designated by the mask, and the marker is set to 0 in the marker cell of every other memory register. This is done almost simultaneously in all the memory registers in one cycle of processing. The ordinary, time-consuming procedure of searching for matching patterns is thus short-circuited.

Our earlier discussion of retrieval with the aid of descriptors and thesauri suggested that searching for matching patterns is likely to be a prevalent operation in procognitive systems. Associative memories are therefore likely to be very useful. However, the simple schema just described is not capable of handling directly the highly complex and derivative associations (e.g., *A* associated with *D* through *B* and *C* if *E* equals *F*) that will be encountered. It seems desirable, therefore, to explore more advanced associative schemata. These should be studied first through simulation on existing computers. Only when the relative merits of various associative-memory organizations are understood in relation to various information-handling problems, we believe, should actual hardware memories be constructed.

In the body of knowledge, relations of high order appear to prevail over simple associations between paired elements. That consideration suggests that we should not content ourselves with simple associative memories, but should press forward in an attempt to understand and devise high-order relational memories.

Develop fast processors consistent with advanced memory structure

Memory, of course, is only part of the picture. With each development in memory structure must come a development in processors. For example, now that "list processing" has been employed for several years, computers are appearing on the market with instruction codes that implement directly most of the manipulations of list structures that were formerly handled indirectly through programming. It will be desirable eventually to have special instructions for manipulating "relational nets" or whatever information structures prove most useful in representing and organizing the fund of knowledge.

*Develop advanced displays and controls
for man-computer interaction*

Some of the projected devices that promise to facilitate interaction between men and the body of knowledge were described on pp. 45–46. Most of the capabilities that were assumed in the example can be demonstrated now, but only crudely, and one feature at a time. It will require major research and engineering efforts to implement the several functions with the required degrees of convenience, legibility, reliability, and economy. Industry has not devoted as much effort to development of devices and techniques for on-line man-computer interaction as it has to development of other classes of computer hardware and software. It seems likely, indeed, that industry will require more special prodding and support in the display-control area than in the other relevant areas of computer technology.

*Develop procedure-oriented, field-oriented,
and user-oriented languages*

The design of special-purpose languages is advancing rapidly, but it has a long way to go. There are now several procedure-oriented languages for the preparation of computer programs (1) to solve scientific problems, (2) to process business data, and (3) to handle military information. Examples are: (1) ALGOL, FORTRAN, MAD, MADTRAN, SMALGOL, BALGOL, and DECAL; (2) COBOL and FACT; and (3) JOVIAL and NELIAC. In addition, there are languages oriented toward (4) exploitation of list processing, (5) simulation techniques, and (6) data bases. Examples are: (4) IPL-V, LISP, KLS, and SLIP; (5) SIMSCRIPT, SIM-

PAC, CLS, MILITRAN, SOL, SIMULA, and GPSS; and (6) ADAM, COLINGO, and LUCID. Finally, there are languages oriented toward the problems of particular fields of research and engineering, for example, STRESS and COGO (for civil engineering), and Sketchpad and APT (for mechanical design).

It will be absolutely necessary, if an effective procognitive system is ever to be achieved, to have excellent languages with which to control processing and application of the body of knowledge. There must be at least one (and preferably there should be only one) general, procedure-oriented language for use by specialists. There must be a large number of convenient, compatible field-oriented languages for the substantive users. From the present point of view, it seems best not to have an independent language for each one of the various processing techniques and memory structures that will be employed in the system, but to embed all such languages within the procedure-oriented and field-oriented languages — as SLIP (for list processing) is embedded within FORTRAN (Weizenbaum, 1963).

Advance the understanding of machine processing of natural languages

To what extent should the language employed in the organization, direction, and use of procognitive systems resemble natural languages such as English? That question requires much study. If the answer should be, "Very closely," the implementation will require much research. Indeed, much research on computer processing of natural language will be required in any event, for the text of the existing corpus is largely in the form of natural language, and the body of knowledge will almost surely have to be converted into some more compact form in the interests of economy of storage, convenience of organization, and effectiveness of retrieval.

In the organization of the corpus, moreover, it will surely be desirable to be able to translate from one natural language to another. Research and development in machine translation is, therefore, relevant to our interests. At present, students of machine translation seem to be at the point of realizing that syntactic analysis and large bilingual dictionaries are not enough, that developments in the field of semantics must be accomplished before smooth and accurate translations can be achieved by machine. Thus machine translation faces the same problem we face in the attempt, upon which we have touched several times, "to organize information into knowledge."

There appear to be two promising approaches to the rationalization of semantics. The first, which we have already mentioned briefly, involves formalization of semantic relations. The second, not yet mentioned, involves (1) the amassing of vast stores of detailed information about objects, people, situations, and the use of words, and (2) the development of heuristic methods of bringing the information to bear on the interpretation of text. As we see it now, researches along both these approaches should be fostered. The first is more likely to lead to compact representations and economic systems. Perhaps, however, only the second will prove capable of handling the "softer" half of the existing corpus.

Develop multiple-access computer systems

The central role, in procognitive systems, of multiple access to large computers was emphasized in an earlier section. It seems vitally important to press on with the

68

development of multiple-console computer systems, particularly in organizations in which creative potential users abound. As soon as it is feasible, moreover, multiple-console computer systems should be brought into contact with libraries. Perhaps they should be connected first to the card catalogues. Then they should be used in the development of descriptor-based retrieval systems. Almost certainly, the most promising way to develop procognitive systems is to foster their evolution from multiple-console computer systems — to arrange things in such a way that much of the conceptual and software development will be carried out by substantive users of the systems.

CHAPTER THREE

Information Storage, Organization, and Retrieval

THE PURPOSE OF this section is to focus briefly on basic concepts of the field of "storage and retrieval" that seem particularly relevant to procognitive systems. Some of the ideas of this field have already been mentioned in our example in which documents were retrieved with the aid of descriptors and a thesaurus. We have also illustrated applications of passage-retrieval and question-answering techniques — techniques that penetrate the covers of documents and deal with sentences and paragraphs or with "ideas" and "facts." Let us now examine those and related techniques a bit more systematically.

The basic unit of knowledge appropriate to our purposes may well be akin to the "idea" of popular and sometime philosophical usage, but we shall not try to exploit that possibility because "idea" is discouragingly nebulous. Alternatively, the basic unit may be closely related to the mathematical concept of "function," or to the logical concept of "relation" that figured centrally in our earlier discussion of relevance networks. Again alternatively, the logical systems of predicate calculus, particularly the so-called higher-order predicate calculi, offer formalisms for the expression of complex attributes (predicates) and attributions (sentences). Some of these systems not only provide implementable procedures for deduction but also have the advantage of being well developed and thoroughly tested. Finally, there is the apparatus of linguistics, with several syntactic categories and myriad rules of grammar.

Despite the ready availability of the foregoing concepts, most of the work that has been done in the field of information storage, organization, and retrieval has been based on the simplest of ideas about sets. The next most popular schema, if we count implicit as well as explicit application, has been geometric space. We may organize our examinations of this area, therefore, by considering storage, organization, and retrieval systems based on the following models: (1) sets and subsets, (2) space analogues, (3) functions and relations, (4) predicate calculus, and (5) other formal languages.

Systems Based on Sets and Subsets

In most systems based on the ideas of sets and subsets, the fundamental concepts are set, partition, item, name, term, prescription, storer, organizer, and retriever, and the logical connectives. Although details of the concepts and the names used in referring to the concepts vary considerably from system to system, the same fundamental ideas appear repeatedly.

The items are the things to be stored and retrieved: documents, facts, and so forth. There is a set of items. Each item may or may not have a name. Terms are associated with items by being written, usually by storers, on the items themselves or on tags or cards associated with the items. Prescriptions are made up mainly of terms and are usually written by retrievers. For each system, there is a rule that determines whether the terms associated with a given document sufficiently match those of a given prescription. The rule and the mechanism for implementing it are devised by organizers. The object of retrieval, in systems based on sets and subsets, is to partition the set of items in such a way as to separate the items a retriever desires from those he does not desire.

In order to establish a perspective, let us examine briefly, and somewhat abstractly, some familiar retrieval schemes.

Partitioning by naming

The very simplest retrieval method achieves the partition by naming the elements (or items) of the desired subset. That method is not applicable to such items as sentences and facts that do not have names. Moreover, when the retriever does not know the names of the items he desires, the method does not work even with those items that do have names, such as books and journal articles. Nevertheless, the method and the location-coded cards often used in implementing it are simple and widely used.

Hierarchical indexing

If the items have no names, or if the names of desired items are unknown to the retriever, it is necessary to fall back on the use of descriptive terms to specify the desired items. In most term-based systems, either it is assumed that the retriever knows the terms, or glossaries or thesauri listing the legal terms of the system are provided. In a hierarchical system, first the over-all set of items is partitioned by organizers into mutually exclusive and exhaustive first-echelon subsets or categories, and a unique term (sometimes a code digit) is assigned to each. Then each first-echelon subset is partitioned into mutually exclusive and exhaustive second-echelon subsets or categories, and a unique term (or code digit) is assigned to each of them. This process of subdivision is continued until there are as many echelons as can be handled conveniently or until there are only a few items in each subset of the lowest echelon. The retriever in this system merely composes a prescription consisting of one term for each echelon. He makes his way down the branching, rootlike structure of the hierarchy, selecting first the first-echelon subset corresponding to the first-echelon term of his prescription, then the second-echelon subset corresponding to the second-echelon term of his prescription, and so forth. When he gets to the bottom, or to a level at which there are not too many items, he examines the items of the subset he has isolated. In practice, the main trouble with this scheme is a trouble inherent in all serial-decision methods: one mistake anywhere in the series, and the game is lost! Perhaps a more basic difficulty is that knowledge does not seem to be naturally susceptible to hierarchical analysis. For these reasons, storage and retrieval systems that set out to be hierarchical often turn into latticelike systems through nonexclusive categorization and cross referencing.

Coordinate indexing

The difficulties just mentioned can be avoided by giving up the notion of precedence that orders the hierarchy. Without precedence, all the subsets and all the terms are coordinate. In coordinate indexing systems, the organizers partition the set of items in various premeditated ways and assign a term, not to each subset, but to each partition. The term itself identifies one of the two subsets separated by the partition — usually the smaller one. (If negation is used, the negation of the term identifies the other subset.) The retriever then draws up a prescription consisting of terms joined by logical connectives. Often the logical "and" is the only connective employed. In some systems, use is made also of "or" and "not." The mechanism that fulfills the prescription has to find and deliver the subset of items corresponding to the logical expression. Given, for example, the prescription:

$$R = A \vee (B \wedge C) \vee (D \wedge \bar{E})$$

the mechanism would retrieve the items characterized by A and those characterized by both B and C, and, in addition, those characterized by D but not by E. Many commercial and government systems are based on coordinate indexing: e.g., most edge-notched-card systems, the Peek-A-Boo Card system, and the descriptor system of the Defense Documentation Center.

Inverse filing

The "natural" or "first-thought" way to set up a coordinate-indexing system with cards is to assign a card to each item and then to record the terms applicable to the item on the card. Second thought, however, may lead to the opposite procedure: assign a card to each term, and record on each card the names or codes of all the items to which the term applies. A file organized the second way is an "inverse" file. Its main advantage is that, since ordinarily there are more items than terms, it requires fewer cards. In the Peek-A-Boo system, each card is divided into many small areas, one for each actual or anticipated item, and an item is associated with a term by punching out the item's area, thus leaving a hole, in the card for the term. When the desired term cards are piled, one on top of another, to form a deck, and are held up to the light, one sees light through the entire deck at the location for each item to which all the terms apply. This is, of course, merely one of several convenient implementations of the logical "and." It illustrates the natural congruence that exists between punched cards and Boolean algebra.

Hybrid systems

Because knowledge has a more complex structure than coordinate indexing can mirror, and still is less perfectly hierarchical than systems based on rootlike branching and exclusive categories must postulate, there have been several efforts to develop hybrid systems that would combine the advantages and avoid the disadvantages of hierarchical and coordinate indexing. One such approach is to employ only a very few echelons of hierarchy and to use coordinate indexing within each echelon. Another is to build a quasi-syntactic structure upon the coordinate-index base by assigning role indicators to the terms. One may distinguish between R_1, wax made by bees, and R_2, bees made of wax, for example, by establishing an *ad hoc* two-echelon hierarchy: (*a*) product, (*b*) source or constituent. In that case we have:

$$R_1 = (a) \text{ wax, } (b) \text{ bees}$$
$$R_2 = (a) \text{ bees, } (b) \text{ wax}$$

Alternatively, one can define the role indicators: $P =$ product, $S =$ source, $C =$ constituent. In that case we have:

$$R_1 = \text{wax } (P), \text{ bees } (S)$$
$$R_2 = \text{wax } (C), \text{ bees } (P)$$

It seems unlikely, however, that such circumventions will lead to highly sophisticated or truly elegant storage and retrieval systems. The fundamental trouble seems to be that elementary set notation and Boolean algebra are inadequate to express compactly the subtle distinctions and intricate relations involved in a sophisticated representation and organization of the body of knowledge. In saying that, however, one should be sure to acknowledge that storage and retrieval systems based on sets and subsets have a particularly strong congruence with present-day information-processing technology and that, despite their limitations in sophisticated applications, they seem to be capable of achieving a high level of effectiveness in document retrieval and even in the retrieval of relevant passages within documents. That is to say, their shortcomings seem likely not to manifest themselves strongly until an effort is made to deduce or infer consequences from the stored representation of knowledge.

SPACE ANALOGUES

The basic notion of topological space analogy is that one item (document, fact, or idea) is the "neighbor" of another item to which it is closely related. Metric space analogy involves the notion of distance in addition to the notion of neighborhood: two items may be close together or far apart, and the distance between them may be analyzed into n components corresponding to the n dimensions of the space.

Metric space analogy is to some extent implicit in the many information-retrieval studies that have used product-moment correlation, multifactor analysis, and related "linear" methods. However, those studies have not emphasized the space concept, and they have led to little or no consensus even about the dimensionality, much less about the identities of the dimensions, of any such thing as "information space" or "semantic space" or "the space of knowledge."

Doubtless the most literal application of the space concept has been Osgood's "semantic differential," based on factor analysis of many human scaling judgments relating linguistic "objects" (such as statements) to named attributive scales (Osgood, Suci, and Tannenbaum, 1957). Osgood and his colleagues have shown, for example, that the same half-dozen basic factors appear in almost all human judgments, and that the fundamental affective dimensions are almost the same the world over — in 16 different ethnolinguistic contexts.* One can see a possibility of relating Osgood's kind of semantic space to the space in which Swanson (1959) has determined correlations among the occurrences of descriptive terms

* C. E. Osgood, Personal communication, March 1963.

and to the space in which Giuliano has determined correlations of the contexts in which descriptive terms occur (Giuliano and Jones, 1963; Giuliano, 1963). However, that possibility has not been developed. There has been much use of methods that assume linearity (and in some instances statistical independence) of the basic variables, but not much explicit discussion of geometric space as a milieu for the representation of knowledge or intellectual processes.

Much of our knowledge deals with the physical world, however, and must be indexed to the physical dimensions of space and time. Place names are in a sense merely spatial coordinates, and linguistic tense has its roots in physical time. It seems difficult, therefore, to conceive of a representation of knowledge within which a geometric framework does not play a major role. How can the attractiveness of the space analogy be reconciled with the obvious merits of logical and linguistic schemata that involve neither geometry nor continuous variables?

The most promising approach, it seems to us, is to accept the notion that, for many years at least, we shall not achieve a complete integration of knowledge, that we shall have to content ourselves with diverse partial models of the universe. It may not be elegant to base some of the models in geometry, some in logic, and others in natural language, but that may be the most practicable solution.

FUNCTIONS AND RELATIONS

Williams, Barnes, and Kuipers (1962) have described an approach to document retrieval based on analysis of natural-language expressions (such as titles) in terms of

78

arguments and functions. In our study, a similar approach was developed in terms of relations.

Functions and relations appear to cover very nearly the same ground. If z is a function F of x and y, which we may write $z = F(x, y)$, then there is a relation R among x, y, and z, and we may write it $R(x, y, z)$. A relation may have any number of arguments. If it has one argument, it is merely an attribute or property. It seems reasonable to say that a single relation, say, $R_{10}(a, b, c, d, \cdots, t)$, might subsume all the interactions described in a long sentence.

The following discussion involves a long example based on a sentence of medium length. The example leads to the statement of a problem and an expression of belief, but not to a solution or a method.

Earlier in this report there appears the sentence: "They will comprise the echelons of the memory hierarchy we have mentioned." If a procognitive system were to try to make sense of that sentence, it would first have to determine the referents of the pronouns. Let us suppose that it is able (with or without human help) to figure out that "they" refers to computer memories that embody various compromises between small-and-fast and large-and-slow, and that "we" refers to the participants in the study, or perhaps to the author together with the readers. The sentence then amounts to the assertion that a complex relation exists among several entities: (a) computer, (b) the memories, (c) time, (d) the echelons, (e) memory, (f) the hierarchy, (g) the participants, (h) comprising, and (i) mentioning.

To take up the matter a small part at a time, in an intuitively guided sequence, we may note first that there

79

is a component relation that is nothing more than a simple qualification (of the common name) of a part of something by associating with it (the common name of) the thing of which it is a part. Thus we have "the computer memories," a relation between (a) and (b) that we may represent as $R_{11}(a, b)$. In "the memory hierarchy," we have another qualification, but of a slightly different kind. The hierarchy is not part of the memory. Instead, the memory is part of the hierarchy, or at any rate memory is the stuff with which the hierarchical structure is filled. We may write $R_{121}(f, e)$, using the common initial subscript to signify the similarity, the distinct second subscript to signify the difference, and the third subscript as a hedge against future complications.

Next let us look at "the echelons" and "the hierarchy." The echelons are abstract parts of the hierarchy. That relation we may call $R_{122}(f, d)$, indicating that it is similar to, and also that it is different from, $R_{121}(f, e)$.

We put the verbs at the end of the list because verbs seem so much like operators and so different from substantives. Nevertheless, let us represent the relation between "time" and "comprising" as $R_3(c, h)$, and the relation between "time" and "mentioning" as $R_4 (c, i)$.

We come now to larger parts of the over-all relation of the sentence. Let us consider "the authors have mentioned," and then let us consider "the memory hierarchy the authors have mentioned." The smaller segment is $R_5[g, R_4(c, i)]$. The larger, which must include some equivalent to the notion that the memory hierarchy is in the main clause whereas the rest is in a dependent clause, is $R_6\{R_{121}(f, e), R_5[g, R_4(c, i)]\}$.

The complex just constructed must mesh with "the

echelons of the memory hierarchy." The two ideas have to fit together in such a way as to indicate that we are planning to move the train of thought forward with the echelons, but that we want to acknowledge that they are parts of a hierarchy, that the nature of the stuff of which the hierarchy is made is memory, and so forth. We may call the abstract meshing relation, together with its nuances, $R_7(x, y)$, and we may make it specific to the sentence in question by substituting the arguments: $R_7\big(R_{122}(f, d), R_6\{R_{121}(f, e), R_5[g, R_4(c, i)]\}\big)$.

Finally, to wind up the example with one big step, we may express the relation among "the computer memories," "comprising" (in the future), and all the rest that we have dealt with as: $R_8\big[R_{11}(a, b), R_3(c, h), R_7\big(R_{122}(f, d), R_6\{R_{121}(f, e), R_5[g, R_4(c, i)]\}\big)\big]$. That formula reflects to some extent the order in which the parts were combined. Since certain other sequences of partial combination would have been equally defensible, it is clear that there are alternative formulas that are equivalent to the one developed.

Now, although the foregoing discussion is ridiculous in several ways, it is instructive in one way and challenging in another. It is ridiculous in that the relational expressions generated are complex and inscrutable, whereas the sentence itself was fairly simple and fairly clear. Unfortunately, it is probably ridiculous also in that we were able to set forth neither a taxonomy of relations nor an algorithm for simplifying the relational expressions. Nevertheless, the relational notation impresses us as much closer to an organizable, processible cognitive structure than is the sentence made of words. Note how much detail there turns out to be in a 12-word sentence. The relational notation makes the detail explicit and manipulable. It challenges us to develop taxonomies and simplification procedures.

Chomsky's (1957) concept of transformational grammars offers a promising approach to both tasks. If Chomsky's methods were fully developed, one could transform any grammatical sentence into canonical form. Some of the information of the original sentence would then reside in a designation of the transformation that was applied, and some would reside in the canonical expression that resulted. On the average, of course, the canonical expression would be simpler and more straightforward than the original.

Even with some of the structural linguistic information factored out, much would remain in the canonical sentence. Some of that information would reside in the syntactic structure; more of it would reside on the nonsyntactic facets of the relations among the elements. Indeed there appear to be at least some thousands of significantly different relations among things. It is not entirely clear that the number is finite, even if we make an engineering interpretation of "significantly different." However, it seems somewhere between conceivable and likely that the myriad and diverse observed relations are compounded of a few dozen — perhaps a hundred — atomic relations, and that the great variety arises when the atoms are combined in ways reminiscent of organic chemistry. If it should turn out to be so, then relational analysis will almost surely be a powerful technique for use in the representation and organization of knowledge.

Our initial thoughts along the line of relational analysis were concerned with relational nets, an example of which is shown in Fig. 4.

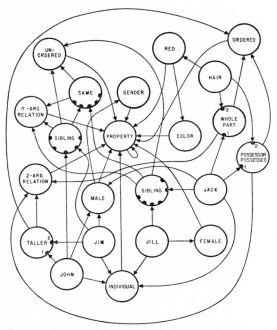

Fig. 4. The diagram represents a relational network. The circles represent entities, relations, and properties. Entities, relations, and properties may participate in relations and have properties. The ultimate property is being a property. The "input terminals" of relations are marked by black spots. Ordered terminals are identified by numbers. Interpretations of the diagram, such as "John and Jim are brothers, and John is taller than Jim" and "Jack has red hair," are explained in the text. We hypothesize that, in a fully developed relevance net of this kind, the alphabetic labels can be erased without loss of any basic knowledge of the situation represented — i.e., without loss of any information other than that rooted in arbitrary selection of unessential symbols.

Consider the circles labeled "John" and "Jim." That they represent individuals is indicated by their connection by arrows to "individual." Individualism — being an individual — is a property, as is shown by the connection from "individual" to "property." Being a property is also a "property," as is shown by the recursive arrow. John and Jim are both male, and they are siblings, therefore brothers. "Sibling" is an n-argument relation, and being an n-argument relation is a property. Every path ends at "property."

There are two "sibling" circles, for one set of siblings uses up a circle, and Jack and Jill are siblings too. As is shown by the arrows from the two "siblings" to "same," being a sibling is the same as being a sibling. "Same" is an unordered, n-argument relation, and "unorderedness" and "n-argumentness" are properties.

"Jack" and his "hair" participate in a whole-part relation and also in a possessor-possessed relation. Both relations have two ordered arguments. The hair is red. Red is a color. Red and color are both properties. Thus Jack has red hair. It is all extremely simple at each step, but there seems to be room for many steps.

As the number of relations and properties grows, the lower-level labels that are not wholly arbitrary can be figured out more and more readily from the higher level labels. In a complete relational net, all the unarbitrary information resides in the structure; the labels (other than the numbers that order the arguments of ordered-argument relations) are entirely superfluous. Relational nets are consequently very attractive as schemata for computer processing.

During the last few months of the library study, Marill (1963) developed the idea of relational nets in the direction of a predicate calculus (see Part II). Marill and Raphael are now simulating net structures on a computer and developing programs that will organize and simplify nets.

PREDICATE CALCULUS

Much of the research during the second year of the study was devoted to question-answering systems. The system constructed by Black, to be described briefly in Part II, was based on the representation of information in the form of statements in first-order predicate calculus. With the information in that form, and with the aid of computer programs designed to process it, the computer could deduce from its information base answers to various questions stated in the formalism (Black, 1963). We believe this to be a significant development. It demonstrates the advantage of employing a formalism that approaches the sophistication and complexity necessary to represent efficiently the subtleties and intricacies of thought and knowledge.

Two other researches are using predicate calculi in ways somewhat similar to Black's. Bohnert,* of the Thomas J. Watson Research Center of I.B.M., is using the first-order predicate calculus. McCarthy,† of Stanford University, is using a second-order predicate calculus that degenerates to first order when time is held constant.

Two severe practical problems are encountered along the path taken by predicate calculus. First, there is as yet no way to translate automatically from statements in natural language to statements in predicate calculus; the translation must be made by people, few people can do it, and the process is time consuming. Second, a small amount of natural language turns into a large amount of predicate calculus. The first problem is, of course, a basic

* H. G. Bohnert, Personal communication, November 1963.
† J. McCarthy, Personal communication, November 1963.

research problem as well as a practical one. The second problem places its demand upon the information technology.

HIGHER-ORDER LANGUAGES

At this stage it seems to be a very good hypothesis that languages of high order are required for compact representation of knowledge, and it seems to be a fairly good hypothesis that such languages are required for efficient processing of knowledge. Even highly complex things *can* be said in very simple languages. For instance, if there were an element in a set for every possible statement, one could make any statement merely by pointing to its element. However, in low-order languages (such as the language of elements, sets, and Boolean operators) the representation of a complex molecule of knowledge is disproportionately voluminous. Our perception of this matter, though still somewhat nebulous, has led us to a rather firm conviction: that the economic and practical advantages of linguistic sophistication are great, and that the intellectual advantage is even greater.

The conviction just set forth is coupled with a second conviction that is less firmly set but is nevertheless a working conviction: in a language to be used in procognitive systems, formality is an extremely valuable asset. Both the lack of formality and the failure to adhere strictly to the rules can cause great difficulties in all kinds of machine processing of information. The problem is not the inconvenience caused by grammatical errors or ambiguities of vocabulary, but rather the high price that civilization pays for the capability that lets man navigate through his sea of syntactic sorrow and semantic confusion. It is almost obvious that man's inability to organize the corpus of his knowledge tightly is due to his having to squander such a wealth of intellectual resource each time he reads a paragraph. For all these reasons we strongly favor the idea of developing high-order formal languages and applying them with machine assistance in organizing the body of knowledge.

Natural English is a high-order language, of course, and, when correctly written or spoken, it may even adhere to a definite form — though surely no one knows quite what the form is. If we try to say what is wrong with English, perhaps we can sharpen the concept toward which we are pointing.

The main shortcoming of English, and presumably of any natural language, is its ambiguity. Natural languages are so often used as adjuncts to nonlinguistic processes that natural languages do not have sufficient chance to practice independence and to develop self-sufficiency. Moreover, when they are exercised in isolation from nonlinguistic processes — in reasoning out solutions to difficult problems, for instance — there is very little opportunity to track down sources of error or confusion. Thus ambiguity persists because it creates no serious difficulty in situations in which the difficulty could be detected and corrected, and ambiguity is rarely detected in situations in which it creates great difficulty. It is no wonder, therefore, that "in" and "of" stand for twenty different relations each, and that "When locked enter through 3D–100" does not tell you what to do when you are locked, nor does it tell you to go through room 3D–100 when the door of 3D–100 is locked.

In short, the trouble with English as a carrier of knowledge is the horrendous amount of calculating on a very large base of data that is expended just to decide which of several locally plausible interpretations of a simple statement is correct or was intended. If the greater part of man's capability is wasted in that kind of processing, he does not have enough left to achieve more significant goals. This conclusion is obvious when the processing of English text is attempted by a present-day computer. It is less obvious but probably just as true for people.

The higher-order language that we propose as an effective carrier for knowledge is a kind of unambiguous English. As long as changes of context are signaled explicitly within the language, no serious problem is introduced by dependence on context. (Indeed, dependence on context appears to be necessary for the achievement of efficiency in diverse special applications.) The proposed language would recognize most or all of the operations, modulations, and qualifications that are available in English. However, it would quantize the continuous variables and associate one term or structure unambiguously with each degree. Finally, the system in which the proposed language is to be implemented would enforce consistent use of names for substantives; it would monitor "collisions" among terms, ask authors for clarifications, and disallow new or conflicting uses of established symbols.

All this advocacy of unambiguous, high-order language may encounter the disdainful accusation, "You're just asking for ruly English!" However, the situation is more favorable now for a ruly version of English than it ever has been, and it will be fully ripe before the new language is likely to be developed. The situation will be ripe, not because people will be ready to adopt a new dialect, but because computers with large data bases will need the new dialect as an information-input language. The envisioned sequence is: from (1) the natural (technical) language of the journal article through a machine-aided editorial translation into (2) unambiguous English, and then through a purely machine transformation into (3) the language(s) of the computer or of the data base itself. At any rate, this is a plausible approach that deserves investigation, though the areas discussed earlier, particularly relational nets and higher-order predicate calculi, will surely provide competitive approaches.

CHAPTER FOUR

Man-Computer Interaction
in Procognitive Systems

IN THE FOREGOING CHAPTERS, the concept of the procognitive system has been approached and developed from several different points of view. Common to these points of view has been the fundamental purpose, to improve the usefulness and to promote the use of the body of knowledge. Also common to the several points of view has been the central methodological theme, that the purpose can best be achieved through intimate interaction among men, computers, and the body of knowledge. Though we shall use the convenient phrase, "man-computer interaction," it should be kept in mind that it is an abbreviation and that the body of knowledge is a coordinate partner of the men and the computers.

In order to come to grips with problems of the projected interaction, it seems necessary to break it down into parts, even though there appears to be no set of components into which the interaction process can be subdivided that do not themselves interact strongly.

The traditional approach, which allocates some functions to men and others to machines, is particularly unsatisfactory because, in order for the major functions involved in working with the body of knowledge to be fulfilled efficiently, synergic action is required in which men and machines participate together. Most of the efforts made during the last decade to figure out "what men should do" and "what machines should do" have missed this point widely. They have supposed that the fabric of man-computer interaction is a patchwork quilt made of red and blue patches, and that the red patches correspond to functions that call only for human capabilities, the blue patches to functions that call only for machine capabilities. In our analysis, however, the fabric of man-computer interaction is an almost uniformly purple quilt, albeit made of red and blue threads. Woven together, they constitute a useful whole. But when one tries to divide it into human functions and machine functions, he winds up not with two sets of assignable tasks but with two tangles of colored thread. By and large, the human threads are heuristic and the machine threads are algorithmic. The art of man-computer system design is the art of weaving the two qualities into solid-color cloth.

Despite the artificiality of division, we shall divide the discussion of man-computer interaction, for convenience, into three parts: (1) what is often called the man-machine interface, the physical medium through which the interactions take place, (2) the language aspects of man-computer interaction, and (3) a look at the total process as an adaptive, self-organizing process. These three sections re-examine some ideas already introduced and fit some new elements into the picture.

THE PHYSICAL "INTERMEDIUM"

Early in our study of man-computer interaction, we became dissatisfied with the term, "man-machine interface." "Interface," with its connotation of a mere surface, a plane of separation between the man and the machine, focuses attention on the caps of the typewriter keys, the screen of the cathode-ray tube, and the console lights that wink and flicker, but not on the human operator's repertory of skilled reactions and not on the input-output programs of the computer. The crucial regions for research and development seem to lie on both sides of the literal interface. In order to remind ourselves continually that our concern permeates the whole medium of interaction, we have avoided "interface" and have used, instead, "intermedium."

The man-computer intermedium subsumes the computer's displays and the mechanisms and programs that control and maintain them, the arrangements through which people communicate information to the computer, and the relevant communication organs and skills of the men. Once we assume that definition of the domain, it is impossible to draw a sharp line between the nonlinguistic and the linguistic parts. The blurred line that we shall in fact draw is intended to put most of the questions of apparatus on one side and to put most of the questions of method, procedure, and format on the other.

An important part of the physical intermedium is the user's station, a "console" of the kind described in an earlier chapter. However, the intermedium extends beyond the console to include the user's entire work space and the physical aspects of his personal documentation system and perhaps even his laboratory system or his application system. We shall not examine those extensions in detail, but that does not mean that we consider them unimportant.

The Oscilloscope-and-Light-Pen Schema

According to the argument set forth in the introduction, it is natural to think in terms of familiar schemata, but it is necessary to abstract from them, or to break them down and recombine them into new configurations, always on the lookout for new elements, if one is to progress. One of the two most flexible and promising display-control systems provided by the current technology is the combination of oscilloscope and light pen that has figured in much of our discussion. That combination is a source of very useful schemata. It is also a source of intense frustration.

Abstracting from the actual physical equipment, and making several improvements and rearrangements in the mind's eye, one comes to a conception that may well be epoch-making as soon as it is well engineered for man's use and widely available. We make this prediction despite the fact that the currently available and familiar equipment has such shortcomings that pencil and paper and the printed page seem to belong to a domain of infinitely superior engineering.

The desiderata are easy to list but probably difficult to achieve. In the following list each item is associated with an intuitive estimate of its degree of importance. The estimate — the number in parentheses — is based on a scale of increasing importance from 0 to 10.

We should like to have: a color display (4) if possible, or, if not, a black-on-white display (7) with at least eight gradations of brightness (5) and a resolution exceeding 400 (4), or 200 (6) or, at any rate, 100 (9) lines per inch. Each element of the display should be selectively erasable by the computer program, and also either directly or indirectly by the operator (9). The display should have controllable persistence (6) and should be free of flicker (9). There should be a way to capture any frame of the display in the form of "hard copy" (9), and the hard copy should be coded automatically for machine filing, retrieval, and redisplay (7).

The display should provide the set of features called "Sketchpad" features (10), which assign to the computer those parts of the sketching and drawing skill that involve much practice and precision, and leave the man responsible mainly for expressing the essential structure of the concept he desires to represent.

The stylus should resemble an ordinary pen or pencil in size, shape, weight, and "feel" (8). It should have a home position slightly above and to the right of the display surface. It should return to that resting place whenever the operator releases it from his grasp. If the stylus is connected by a wire to the console, the wire should be very light and flexible and should not constrain the manipulation of the stylus.

In addition to the foregoing considerations, there are, of course, reliability (9), ruggedness (8) and economic feasibility (10). The challenge inherent in the last three factors sometimes seems to be too little appreciated.

The oscilloscope-and-light-pen schema of the next

decade should have a hard, tough surface upon which both the user and the computer can print, write, and draw, and through which the user's markings will be communicated to the computer. Even when this surface is flush with the top of a desk, no "electron gun" sticks down through the desk and bumps the user's knees. The marks appear on the surface, of course, and not on a lower subsurface: there is no explosion screen and no parallax.

Ideally, the user and the computer should make their marks in precisely the same coordinate frame, so that it will not be necessary to compensate for poor registration. It is easy and natural to designate part of an observed pattern by pointing to it or touching it directly with fingertip or stylus. Since the computer must act upon designations made by the pointing or touching of patterns displayed on the screen, it seems to us important to have the frame of reference for sensing correspond precisely to the frame of reference for displaying. It may be easier to develop equipment in which the user and the computer make their marks on separate screens, but whether that is a satisfactory arrangement should be evaluated carefully.

A device called the RAND Tablet* has been developed which will provide experience with separate display surfaces for man and computer. The RAND Tablet looks to the user like a sheet of paper. Underneath the paper, however, there is a layer of insulating material on each surface of which are a thousand or more parallel conductive lines. The lines run from right to left on one

---

* The RAND Tablet is similar in principle to a device invented by H. M. Teager of M.I.T. Both devices involve conductive lines and coded pulses. The path from the lines to the stylus is capacitive in the RAND Tablet and inductive in the Teager Table.

surface of the insulating sheet and from front to back on the other. Coded patterns of pulses are applied to the various conductive lines by a pulse generator. When the user touches his stylus to the paper, the stylus picks up the pulses from the nearest conductive lines and transmits them, by way of a connecting lead, to electronic circuits associated with the pulse generator. These circuits determine the location of the tip of the stylus and transmit the coordinates to the computer. Because the conductive lines are produced in the same way as printed circuits, the Tablet is not very expensive. Doubtless, the electronic circuits that generate the coded pulses and determine the location of the stylus can eventually be produced at low cost as "integrated circuits."

The Tablet handles only the problem of communication from the user to the computer and does not provide a display from computer to operator. At the RAND Corporation, the Tablet is used in association with a computer-posted oscilloscope display. The Tablet is mounted flat on the writing surface of the console. The screen of the oscilloscope is vertical and located immediately behind the Tablet. On the basis of early experience, the RAND people say that the separation of the computer's display from the user's Tablet is not a source of serious difficulty.

A working version of another component of the schema we have been discussing is provided by the "flat" cathode-ray tube. Whereas an ordinary cathode-ray tube has the (often inconvenient) shape of an Erlenmeyer flask, the flat tube has the shape of a book. Operable flat oscilloscopes have been constructed and have proved to afford excellent resolution.

In several military display systems, projection of photographic "slides" is combined with display generation by computer. The slides provide a convenient and economical way of maintaining the static part of the display pattern, which is often a reference grid or a map. A few of the systems provide means for photographing computer-posted displays and then redisplaying the information from slides. We think that, should such an arrangement be produced at low cost, it would find widespread use (7) in procognitive systems.

The typewriter schema

The second main area in which improvement of controls and displays is required is the area of alphanumeric keyboards and hard-copy displays. Those devices are obviously important for the future of procognitive systems.

The main functions to be fulfilled by devices derived from the typewriter schema are obvious ones. Such devices must provide for "digital" communication from the user to the computer. They must also provide a visible record of the information that has been fed into the computer, and this record should be easy to modify. The computer should be able to make marks on the record. The user should have the option of producing either soft (ephemeral) copy or hard (permanent) copy, and even the option of turning the soft copy into hard copy after editing. The device should accept input as fast as a well-trained operator can provide it, and it should translate signals from the computer into typed characters at a rate of at least 100 characters per second.

The typewriterlike devices that are currently available provide five schemata that are useful as bases for thinking in this area. Let us abstract from these schemata the parts and qualities we should like to have melded together for use in procognitive systems.

The first schema is offered by the familiar teletypewriter. Although there are several models of teletypewriter, the general features are sufficiently characteristic that, for some of our purposes, we may think simply of "the" teletypewriter. Compared to most other man-computer communication devices, it is rugged, reliable, and inexpensive. However, it has no lower-case letters, it is slow, and it has a strange "touch" for anyone accustomed to office typewriters. Many people who have had experience with on-line man-computer interaction look forward to the manufacture of a device like current models, but with 128 or more characters, with the capability of typing at very high speed, and with a touch more like that of an ordinary electric typewriter. We realize, however, that, in the present state of the art, these features are to a large extent incompatible with high reliability and low cost.

The schema offered by the familiar electric typewriter, or by the electric typewriter that has been designed or adapted to be used with a computer, is a montage of 44 type keys, six to twelve operation keys, two cases, fairly clear marks on paper in one or two colors, limited control of the carriage from the keyboard, fair reliability, and a high level of noise. The ensemble of 88 characters (2 cases × 44 keys) is almost large enough for serious intellectual purposes. The font contains both capital and lower-case letters. These things are important. Perhaps even more important are the intimate familiarity with typewriters and the significant skill in typing that are fairly widespread in the population.

It is worth pausing to ponder how few well-developed

skills there are that are both complex and widespread. Almost everyone can get about in three-dimensional space. Almost everyone can speak and understand one of the natural languages — perhaps not grammatically, but fluently. But relatively few people can do anything else that is even remotely comparable in informational complexity and degree of perfection. Of the remaining candidates for inclusion in the list of widespread complex skills, we may with some misgivings accept writing, and perhaps the playing of musical instruments. After this comes typing. And typing ends the list. It is possible that, in future decades, typing will move up past music and that it will become almost as widespread as writing and more highly developed.

The third typewriter schema is offered by typewriter-like devices that are used in association with computers and that type 60 or more characters per second. These are usually called "printers." (We refer here to character printers and not to line printers, which are likely to remain too complex and expensive for ordinary user stations.) The aspect of the printer schema that is of interest is simply the rapid rate of typing. It is worth while to have in mind that characters *can* be marked on paper at high speed by a device the size of a typewriter.

The fourth schema is offered by devices commercially available but not in widespread use, separated keyboards and typing units. When a typewriter is associated with a computer, there ceases to be any reason for the conventional, direct connection between the key that is pressed and the type bar that strikes the paper. Obviously the pressing of the key should direct a code to the computer, and the computer should acknowledge the code by activating the type bar and thus printing the character on the paper. As soon as the tacit assumption of a direct linkage between key and type bar is recognized and discarded, there is no longer any need to maintain a one-to-one relation between key pressings and character markings. It should be possible, in a "debreviation" mode, to type "clr" on the keyboard and have "The Council on Library Resources, Inc." appear on the display.

The final schema in the typewriter field is the "Stenotype." The component that seems to be of most value, for these purposes, is simultaneous multiple key pressing. If it turns out, as seems likely, that very large ensembles of characters are desirable in man-computer interaction with the body of knowledge, then it will become much more important than it is now to be able to specify the desired character by pressing a pattern of keys on a small keyboard. That is a much better solution than pressing a single key on a keyboard with several thousand keys.

Displays for group-computer interaction

Because our thinking is anchored in familiar experiences, we are inclined to think of interaction between men and procognitive systems as a collection of dyadic man-computer interactions. More and more, however, the problems of science, technology, industry, and government are being solved by groups of men rather than by individuals. Although the "team approach" is a topic of controversy in some fields, its value has been proven in others. Consideration should be given to the development of tools and techniques to facilitate group interaction with the body of knowledge.

In the current technology there are two general approaches to group-computer interaction. The first and most widely used provides a separate console for each member of the group and relies upon the computer, together with auxiliary communication circuits, to mediate the interaction among the members of the group as well as the interaction of the members with the computer and its store. The second approach, taken in some military systems, uses large "wall" displays, located in view of several or all of the members of the group and intended to provide a common frame of reference for their decisions and actions.

In procognitive systems based on individual consoles, the main items of equipment that would be needed for group communication, not already discussed under the heading of man-computer communication, would be derivatives of the telephone and television. Communication by telephone and perhaps by television would be closely correlated with communication through the computer system. This procedure does not pose any novel requirements for the display and control equipment of the system.

In a procognitive system with group displays (second approach) one would expect to see large-scale displays similar in principle to the individual display screen already discussed, even with derivatives of the light pen to provide communication between the human members of the team and the computer. The most significant characteristic of the group display seems to us to be resolution. The total number of resolvable points is no greater in the large-scale kinematic displays available at present than it is in the smaller individual displays. In some large-scale static displays, such as wall maps, however, there is high resolution, and in them the advantage of size is apparent. On a good wall map, one can see the general features of a continent from the middle of the room. In order to examine the boundaries of countries or states, it is necessary only to step a little closer. From a normal reading distance, the names of cities and towns can be made out and the courses of rivers can be followed. It is interesting to extrapolate to very high resolution and dynamic presentation. If display capabilities should increase as rapidly as memory capabilities, one may someday watch a display on a very large wall, examine the weather situation in the Midwest, and then with a magnifying glass follow the movement of an individual automobile from Bethesda to the Pentagon, reading the names of the streets and highways along which it moves. It seems to us that there is some merit in trying to develop such large-scale, high-resolution dynamic displays for group-computer interaction, though at the same time we appreciate the difficulty of the technical problems involved.

Consoles and work spaces

The design of consoles and the arrangement of work spaces is not likely to be regarded as an exciting part of library planning, but it is an essential step in overcoming what C. W. Churchman calls the "brain-desk barrier." During the course of our experience with facilities for man-computer interaction, the point was driven home to us that convenient arrangement of the elements of the physical intermedium is an extremely important factor in the determination of the effectiveness of the interaction and not something readily purchased or easily achieved. The individual ingredients of the current difficulty of man-computer interaction are trivial in themselves, but they add up to a significant total.

The first inconvenience is likely to be the position of

102

the keyboard of the computer typewriter. Most computer typewriters are located on "console" desks that are higher than typewriter tables. The keyboards of most computer typewriters stand higher above their resting surfaces than the keyboards of ordinary typewriters do. That makes the keyboard much too high. Raising the chair seat makes the typist's knees hit the table. Moving the computer typewriter to a conventional typewriter table puts the typewriter too far away from the oscilloscope screen, the light pen, and the switches that control the computer.

In the computer-posted displays that we have seen, the oscilloscope screen stands only 10 or 20 degrees off the vertical. This is true for displays that have light pens associated with them as well as for screens that function only as displays. Evidently, the designers had in mind the blackboard and not the writing desk. In fact, one's blackboard habits carry over to the vertical oscilloscope screen, and one writes and draws in a large scale inappropriate to the small size and high resolution of the display. Moreover, it is tiring to hold a hand at eye height for a long time without support.

The other elements of difficulty are of the same general nature: Light pens are too thick and heavy for facile writing; they could be and should be the size and weight of ordinary pens. Conventional "line printers" have no lower-case letters; it is difficult to read long passages in capital letters. One has to turn the lights out to read the oscilloscope and then turn them back on to read print or typescript. And so forth. Each individual difficulty can be remedied easily, but it may take a strong, well-organized effort to perfect all the necessary elements and combine them into an effective physical intermedium.

MAN-COMPUTER INTERACTION LANGUAGES

If the problems of the physical intermedium of man-computer interaction are lacking in intellectual challenge, the problems of language for man-computer interaction abound in it. The entire spectrum of language from binary machine code to the great natural languages will be involved in man's interaction with procognitive systems.

We may distinguish four different involvements of language in a neolibrary procognitive system. Language is employed (1) by the programmers who prepare and improve the computer programs that implement the basic operations of the system; (2) by the information specialists who endeavor continually to improve the organization and operation of the system; (3) by the substantive users of the system in their interaction with the body of knowledge; and (4) in the representation of the body of knowledge in the memory of the system.

The science of applied linguistics is so new, and formal languages designed to facilitate the programming of computers are burgeoning so fast, that it is difficult to summarize the present situation and almost impossible to make a long-term projection worthy of confidence. This part of the discussion, therefore, is confined to a brief examination of the roles of language in the four areas of man-computer interaction.

Programming language

Even after it has been developed and is in operation, the procognitive system of the year 1994 has a continuing need for programming specialists. Their task is, essentially, to maintain and improve the basic programs of the system. Requirements arise that cannot be met effectively without making alterations in the basic system programs. To change even one short statement in a large system of programs is a serious matter, to be undertaken only by the most skilled and experienced professional programmers. The programmers of the procognitive system, therefore, plan modifications carefully, test them thoroughly outside the main stream of operation of the system, and then monitor the situation closely when they introduce the modifications into actual operation.

Basic programs for the procognitive system are written in a high-level programming language. The programs are available to anyone who wishes to examine or use them, not only as services that will function at the user's request, but also in the form of annotated statements in the programming language. When a system programmer modifies a system program, he operates upon it through another program designed to facilitate the preparation, testing, modification, documentation, storage, and retrieval of programs. This "programming-system" program provides several separate services, each of which can be brought into operation by simply typing its name. Each service makes available to the programmer a specialized language attuned to its own structure and functions. Together with his physical intermedium, the programming languages guide and implement the programmer's interaction with the system.

Let us observe a programmer at work, modifying a basic graphical display program in order to make it operate with a new display device that provides eight times as much linear resolution as the older "standard" displays provide. We shall concentrate more on the functions and operations than on the syntax and terminology.

The programmer sits down at his console, turns it on,

and calls the programming system. It reports for service, and he requests the program retrieval and editing program. It reports, and he asks it for the names of all the screen-display programs that are regularly used. Of the 20 offered, he selects four as likely to include the one he must change, and he asks to see their abstracts. From the abstracts, he selects one and asks to see its listing in the high-level language in which it was written. From the listing, he can tell almost at once that he has the program he wants, for the listing is heavily annotated, and it is immediately clear that the number of lines in each scan is the familiar number and that the division of the screen into sectors is the same as the one currently in use throughout the system.

Using the "moving window" * to scan through the program, the programmer gets an over-all picture of the display routine and then returns to its beginning, where he finds a statement labeled "Interrogate display" and a comment to the effect that, through interrogation, the program checks the type designation of the screen on which it will display information. Such a check is made because at one time or another several different types of display have been in the system. What is being introduced is a fifth or sixth type. The programmer figures out that the result of the interrogation is a code, that the first ten digits of the code are checked against a standard to provide authentication, and that the last four digits of the code are used as the argument of a "transfer-table" or "jump-table" operation. He therefore temporarily dismisses the entire programming system, calls a document-

---

* A "moving window" display that lets the programmer see a selectable and variable segment of program or data in the computer memory has been demonstrated by Marvin Minsky and associates at M.I.T.

retrieval program, and retrieves the engineering specification of the new display device. He looks at the document long enough to satisfy himself that he has the correct display program. He then asks the question-answering system the identification code of the display described in the document. Just as the question-answering system is displaying the answer, he finds the passage in the document that gives the code. He makes sure that the two displays of the code are identical. He sees that the last four bits are 1101 (decimal 13). He makes a note of that and recalls the programming system, which comes back into action with the retrieval and editing program operating in the mode in which he last used it.

The programmer notes next that the name of the transfer table is "Display-selector transfer table." He types:

```
Insert in Display-selector transfer table
+ 13 a jump to Patch.  Prepare Patch:
Deposit in user's scratch-pad register
(Insert here designation of user's
scratch-pad area used in the first deposit
operation following the jump-out from
Display-selector transfer table + 12) the
octal constant [Insert here (the octal
constant inserted in last-cited deposit
operation)/10].
```

Then on the next line he types:

```
Jump to the return used by Display-
selector transfer table + 12.
```

Then finally he asks to see a screen display of the newly prepared patch program. In the first register of the patch, the programming system has composed the instruction "Deposit," the octal constant "4000," and the symbolic address "Scratch-pad area, Display + 6." In the next register it has deposited the instruction "Jump" and the symbolic address "Initialize display." Seeing this, our programmer thinks a moment about the "4000" and decides that it is a plausible value for the constant. He then types:

```
Display "Initialize display".
```

and looks at the part of the program to which the "Jump" leads. The program statements in that segment seem appropriate to him. He therefore decides to test the modified program.

The modification has been so short and simple that he sees no reason to test it under "trace," which would have the effect of running it slowly and protecting other programs against interference in the event that it should misbehave. However, it does occur to him to take one more precaution before testing. He decides to give the patch a retrievable label (to replace the local, nonretrievable label, "Patch") and to store away a copy of the modified program so that he can retrieve it and work on it further if the test is unsatisfactory. He therefore types:

```
Assign the label, "Constant for display
13" to the statement locally labeled
"Patch".
```

The programming system pauses a moment and then replies:

The label, "Constant for display 13", has already been used.

It occurs to him immediately what the trouble is, and he types:

```
Assign "Constant for display 13, H. I.
Johnson".
```

The programming system then replies:

Done.

108

In order to test the program, the programmer takes advantage of a substitution technique provided by the testing part of the programming system. He calls for the testing service and then asks to have a set of test data displayed on his old display screen, which is still connected. As soon as he has confirmed that the data are displayed on his old display screen, he substitutes one of the new display devices for his old one and requests the test program to substitute the program he has just modified for the regular program. The system will effect the substitution as soon as it comes to the part of the regular program that matches (except for the modification) the part he has just modified. This is a fairly complicated operation, but it is easier and surer for the system to find the place where the substitution should be effected than it is for the programmer to specify it precisely. The programmer then calls for a redisplay of the data. This time the data show up on his new display, the format is the same, the resolution is better, and everything seems to be working well.

Now the programmer acts on the insight he had achieved a minute or two earlier — the realization that one or more than one other programmer has been working on the modification, programming it in parallel with him, so that two or more versions of the modification can be compared before the modification is introduced into the operating system. He therefore asks the programming system:

```
Is another programmer modifying a screen-
display program?
```

The programming system says that no one is working on such a modification now, but that O. B. Smith worked on one earlier in the day. Our programmer asks to talk with O. B. Smith. The system makes the connection. The two programmers discuss their modifications on the telephone. Each calls for both versions of the modified program in order to check that they are identical in their essentials. It turns out that O. B. Smith had happened upon the label, "Constant for display 13," only an hour or two earlier than H. I. Johnson and had thereby set up the collision of labels that had been detected by the system.

The two versions of the program do match, except in respect of arbitrary labels. The two programmers together delete the retrievable patch label. They enter a note in the system log, indicating that they have made a modification and giving its location, purpose, and nature, and their names and the date. Then they replace the old program with the modified program in the system files and in the operating system. In that final step they use — without stopping to think about it — a sophisticated capability of the system. Before substituting the modified version for the old one, the system checked to see that no one was at the moment in the process of using the old one.

In the foregoing account, attention was focused on the programming system and the language and procedure used in modifying a program — not on the programming language in which the system programs were originally written. There is little to say about the basic programming language except that it is a powerful and sophisticated descendent of present-day computer-programming languages and the product of long-continued, intensive research.

The example was intended to illustrate how closely

interwoven are the threads of hardware, system design, programming technique, and programming language. It touched also upon the capability of the programming system to interrelate the efforts of members of the system programming team.

Organizing language

The system specialists in their continual effort to improve the organization of the body of knowledge and the usefulness of the procognitive system must deal with a variety of languages and procedures. Whereas the language of the programming system dealt with programs written in a consistent, high-level programming language, the "organizing language" dealt with documents written in the various natural languages, with mathematical models and computer-program models, with computer programs themselves, and — most intensively — with large, coherent systemizations of knowledge represented in the "representation language" that constitutes the foundation of the question-answering system. Associated with each of these diverse objects is a set of information structures and procedures with which the organizing language must resonate. Therefore, the organizing language is divided into parts, any one of which may be brought into play almost instantly by any one of the system specialists who can direct it on the task with which he is concerned.

One of the main tasks of the system specialists is to transfer information from the document store associated with a subfield of knowledge to the organized body of knowledge of that subfield. This operation involves, but is not wholly restricted to, translation from natural language to the representation language. We say that it is not wholly restricted to such translation because many of the documents entering the procognitive system consist mainly of metainformation and are intended not to express substantive findings so much as to set such findings (represented in auxiliary structures) into relation with problems, to define their scopes and domains, and to offer qualifications and suggestions about their applications and their correlation with the body of knowledge. The substantive findings are typically expressed in the form of a high-order formal language, or in the form of operable computer programs ("dynamic models"), or in the form of data structures such as lists, tables, and matrixes. The fact that the incoming information is already to a large extent formalized and organized simplifies the problem for the system specialist. During the future period to which this discussion refers, many scientists are beginning to use in their own work the formal language in terms of which the body of knowledge is represented in the procognitive system. However, the rapid advance in the understanding of languages and the burgeoning of linguistic techniques and formalisms are still in progress, and the time when one great formal language will dominate procognitive intercourse appears still to be decades away.

The organizing language contains a section that handles translation from natural language to the representation language. This section provides translators for each of the main natural languages. These translators work in both directions. One of the major items of routine business is to translate a document into the formal representation language, then to translate it back into a long series of short statements in the natural source language, and then to review the new version in a conference with the author of the document. The system specialists who handle that part of the work are educated in the scientific or technical disciplines they deal with, as well as in the information sciences.

The process of translation is carried out mainly by algorithm, but, even after two decades of progress, there are still many problems and difficulties that must be solved or circumvented by human specialists. The problem of capturing and representing precisely the intention of an author is still so difficult that the conference between the specialist and the author of a 10-page paper may take as much as an hour. By the time the conference is finished, however, the natural-language text has been perfected to the point at which it can be translated into the representation language without the loss of any information the author considers essential. When the translation algorithms operate upon the final natural-language text, they ordinarily require no human intervention. Whenever a problem of translation persists, however, it is made the subject of a conference between the system specialist and experts who specialize in translation algorithms. Over the years, these conferences have contributed much to the perfection of the translation algorithms.

In this part of the work the language employed by the system specialist is essentially a language for controlling the operation of language algorithms, editing text (jointly with a colleague at a distant console), testing the logical consistency of statements in the representation language, and checking the legality of information structures and formats. The part of the language concerned with editing is to a large extent graphical. Both the system specialist and the author point to words and sentences in the text, move them about with the aid of their styli, insert or substitute new segments of text, and so forth. The language used in controlling algorithms is essentially standard throughout the procognitive system.

When an incoming document contains many references to associated information structures, the task of the system specialist expands. He has to introduce the links that will connect the textual document with the associated structures and the associated structures one with another. Inasmuch as the work we are discussing is done in a second-echelon center, this does not involve the actual introduction of the new information into the over-all body of knowledge, but — operation for operation — it amounts to almost the same thing. The main difference is that there is even more caution, more insistence upon verification in the top-echelon centers. In linking the various structures, the system specialist makes statements of the following kind:

```
Table 3 is a two-dimensional matrix with
alphanumeric row and column headings and
with row and column marginal totals.  The
entries are floating-point decimal num-
bers.  Check the format.  If it is all
right, file it, and construct a bidirec-
tional link to "Table 3" and the title.
```

The system will know, of course, to file it in the data base.

Encountering a series of equations in a document, and seeing that they are sufficiently complete to constitute an operable computer routine, the system specialist makes a series of commands such as the following:

```
Assign an arbitrary PROCOL independent
routine label to these [He points] equa-
tions.  Construct a bidirectional link
between the text and the routine.  Assume
```

114

```
ranges for the variables.  Assume assign-
ments of variables to axes.  Display rela-
tions on screen while running program.
Run the routine.
```

In this way, the system specialist checks the operability of the system of equations as a "PROCOL routine." While observing the display, he may, for example, make some modifications in the ranges of variables, and substitute z for x as the independent variable. In such operations, he uses the graph-control sublanguage that is standard for the entire procognitive system.

One of the main features of the language mechanism used by the system specialist is a built-in "understanding" of the several kinds of information structure that system specialists usually handle. When the information structure is a matrix, certain operations, certain storage locations, certain kinds of link, certain kinds of test, and certain kinds of display are appropriate. When the information structure is an operable program, a different set of things is appropriate. When the information structure is a textual string, still different things are appropriate. The linguistic development that has made all this possible has been the development of an interpretive mechanism that examines the class memberships of the entities mentioned in the declarations, commands, and questions, determines from those memberships what operations and interrelations are appropriate and uses that information to guide its implementation of the instructions.

The format of the illustrative commands given in the foregoing paragraphs is intended, of course, only to suggest. No such language is currently implemented on a computer. The suggestion is that such a language will in due course be implementable. The use of pronouns will

115

cause no serious difficulty. Most of the power of the language stems from the interplay of the facts already mentioned, (1) that the language mechanism "understands" the information structures that will be encountered in its work, and (2) that the operations to be performed upon the information structures have been carefully programmed and associated with the verbs of the language.

The design of a specialized language, according to this line of thinking, is in large part a matter of identifying the information structures and the fundamental operations of the special domain of application. It includes also the formulation of a sufficiently sophisticated syntactic analysis to permit flexibility of expression and sensitiveness of response to tense, voice, mood, and so forth. The language must, of course, be intimately correlated with the physical intermedium and with the repertory of processing techniques that are available. "Techniques," as used here, is not the same as "operations." There may be several different ways to carry out a given operation. To the substantive user, the difference may appear only in speed or in cost. To the system specialist or the programmer, on the other hand, the selection of a particular technique may have profound implications. Selecting the wrong technique for the performance of a fundamental operation might seriously handicap future development of the system. One of the main responsibilities of system specialists, therefore, is to exercise good judgment about the selection of techniques. The selection of operations, on the other hand, is determined largely by the requirements of the task at hand.

We have discussed one particular kind of task in which system specialists are involved. Let us now turn to another kind of task. It is part of what we have called "mulling over" the body of knowledge — looking for undetected relations within it and for possibilities of improving its organization. Let us concern ourselves here with one small facet of that endeavor.

Consider the work of a system specialist who is exploring the possibility that there may exist, within a part of the body of knowledge as currently represented, a number of basic abstract correlations that have not yet been detected. Let us suppose that he has available the language and processing mechanisms capable of transforming patterns of information from the standard representation language into various other representations, based upon other information structures. By "information structures," we refer, of course, to trees, lists, matrixes, relational nets, semantic nets, multidimensional space analogues, and so forth. The foregoing are currently available examples, but during the next decades there should be great development — both in proliferation and in sophistication — of information structures.

The language employed by the system specialist handles the standard representation language approximately the way a present-day query language handles a simple hierarchical file. The system specialist might say, for example:

```
Designate as A, B, and C, respectively,
the parts of the representation that con-
tain models involving DNA and RNA, models
of transformational grammars, and
information-compression codes.  Transform
each of the parts, A, B, and C, into
"trie" representation, list-structure
representation, and semantic-net represen-
tation.  Within each of the latter,
truncate each representation tentatively,
retaining the highest-level 1,000,000
```

117

bits. Now, consider subdivisions of the
representation that are locally complete
and approximately 10,000 bits in size.
Correlate all the subrepresentations of A
with each subrepresentation of B, and do
the same for B and C and for C and A.
Display all pairs of patterns that have
correlations greater than 0.8.

In the foregoing series of commands (which in practice would have been interspersed with requests for step-
by-step display of results), there were many points at
which substantive knowledge of information structures
and technical operations had to be "understood" by the
language mechanism. Since many of the structures and
most of the operations are of particular significance to
system specialists, the organizing language contains specific terms for them.

System specialists have many other tasks besides the
two that have been discussed. They preside over the introduction, into the top-echelon representation of the
body of knowledge, of those contributions that are locally
organized and tested in the second-echelon centers. They
call to the attention of experts in the various substantive
fields the correlations and systematizations they find
plausible in their continual examination of the body of
knowledge, and they work with the substantive experts
in reorganizing the representations of substantive areas.
They seek continually to improve the representation language. Approximately once each decade they have to
adapt the representation to a new and improved hardware base. In so doing, they work closely with the system
programmers. Indeed, there are some system specialists
who are programmers, and some programmers who are
system specialists. There is no sharp line between the two,

any more than there is a sharp line between system specialists and specialists in substantive areas of science and technology.

User-oriented languages

The existence of so very many subfields of science and technology, each with its local jargon, its own set of frequently occurring operations, and its own preferences for data structures and formats, makes it necessary to have many different user-oriented languages. However, there is a homogeneity that underlies the diversity. We have seen the basis for this underlying homogeneity in our discussion of programming language and organizing language. The homogeneity is inherent in the fact that there are only a few syntactic classes, only a few dozen information structures, and only about a hundred *kinds* of operation — though there are very many different operations — in the entire spectrum of activities of the procognitive system. The various field-oriented and problem-oriented languages employed by the substantive users of the system are therefore all related, one to another, and they are similar in their basic essentials to the languages used by the programmer and the system specialist.

One of the tasks of the specialist that is relevant in the present connection is to keep the user-oriented languages compatible with one another. User-oriented languages naturally tend to develop in their own particular directions, and every effort is made not to impede such development when the needs are truly special. It usually turns out, however, that consultation between a substantive user and a system specialist reconciles achievement of the goal of a new specialization with preservation of order within the over-all system. This is true because the substantive user only rarely invents a new linguistic technique that is superior, for his purposes, to every other technique already established within the system and because any new and useful one that he does invent soon finds application in other parts of the system.

The interaction between a substantive user and the procognitive system may be intellectually as deep as the user's penetration of his field of study, but it should be simple. It tends to be simple because there are only a few kinds of action for the user to take at his console. Almost everything posted on a display, for example, is put there by the computer. If the user wants to make a mark or turn on a light, he tells the computer what, when, and where, and the computer proceeds to carry out the act.

In order to match the small set of control actions a man can take with the vast assortment of things there are to be done in the world of the procognitive system, it is necessary to take advantage of the concept of determination by local context that is so highly developed in the natural languages. In the system of user languages, the first step in that direction is the selection of a sublanguage — a field-oriented or problem-oriented language designed to handle the kind of task with which the user is concerned. The second step, taken within the sublanguage, is to enter a "mode." We have already touched briefly on modes of display associated with the display screen and the light pen. When the pen is used merely as a pointer, the meaning of its message is conveyed partly by the location of the spot to which it points. However, the meaning is determined also by the nature of the display that is currently being presented and the particular details of that display. The part of the determination that is associated with the nature of the display is "mode" determination.

The simplest on-line man-computer interaction systems we know of have only two modes: a "control mode" and a "communication mode." In the control mode, the signals the operator directs to the computer select one or another of a set of subprograms. In the communication mode, the signals merely enter a buffer space in the computer's memory, and what the computer then does to the signals depends upon which subprogram is brought into action. For example, in an on-line "debugging" system called "DDT," the programmer, trying to find out what is wrong with his program, might type:

sto/

The solidus is a control-mode signal that means "I have just transmitted to you three characters or their equivalent that constitute the label of a register in memory. When you have received them, look them up in your address table, examine the register with the corresponding address, and type out in octal notation the number you find in it." In response, DDT would type the number:

sto/ 123456

If the programmer wanted to change that number to 123321, he would simply type 123321 and press the carriage-return key. The carriage return is another control character. It says, "Substitute the number now in the buffer for the old one, and do nothing else about this register unless it is mentioned to you again." The programmer might then check to see that the new number had in fact replaced the old. To make the check, he would press the period key and the solidus key. (The period is not a control character. It is a "pronoun" that stands for the last-mentioned register label.) The computer would then respond with the number in the second line:

```
sto/        123456    123321
./          123321
```

It is evident from the foregoing that DDT uses a shorthand notation that is much less explicit than the notations used in the examples given in connection with programming language and organizing language. This is partly because the language of DDT is not very far removed from machine code, whereas the hypothetical languages are high-level languages. Nevertheless, there is an advantage to the terseness of the DDT control language that should not be lost to increasing sophistication. This matter will be discussed in the section on Representation Language. The point here is that one part of what the user types is essentially an instruction to the system, telling it what to do to an object, and another part is the object on which the system is to act. This fundamental distinction will probably never disappear. However, it will not long remain as simple as it is in DDT.

One of the first necessary complications of the distinction between the control mode and the communication mode has already appeared in several on-line languages and is also found in DDT. It is the "execute" command. The execute command instructs the system to consider the object communicated no longer as an object to be processed but as a command to be implemented. The computer therefore executes the communicated message as an instruction. This corresponds approximately to removing the quotation marks from a string of characters of ordinary text. Several groups have recently built into

ALGOL the capability of removing the quotation marks from a string of characters and executing the string as an ALGOL procedure.

We may expect a continual development of on-line interaction languages until the residual distinction between control and communication mode is carried partly by the syntactic structure of statements and partly by context. In the work with programs discussed earlier, for example, the system programmer first examined the programs, treating them as objects, and then tested them, causing the system actually to carry out the procedures.

The convenience of having local context or mode implicitly define terms and particularize procedures for him may to some extent be countered by the responsibility, thrust upon the user, of continually keeping track of the prevailing mode. However, one of the basic facts of man-machine interaction is that, although the responsibility for keeping track of mode or situation causes great difficulty in monitoring, it causes almost no difficulty in truly symbiotic interaction. In truly symbiotic interaction, the human partner is always active, always involved in directing, always "ahead of the game." In monitoring, on the other hand, he tends just to sit there, waiting for an alarm to alert him to action. When the alarm goes off, he does not know what the situation is, and it is difficult or impossible to find out in time to do anything effective. It does not help the monitor much to display to him the developing situation, either in summary or in detail, for it is almost impossible for him to think ahead constantly if his thinking has no effect on what happens. In our conception of man-computer interaction in procognitive systems, however, the man is no mere monitor. He is a partner — indeed he is usually the dominant, leading partner.

On-line interaction introduces into the language picture the possibility of "conversation." This possibility, together with the need to bring on-line languages abreast of conventional programming languages, opens an inviting field to research and development. It seems to us desirable to move rapidly beyond the simple dichotomy between the control and communication modes and to develop a syntax in which it will be possible to express commands, state facts, and ask questions in any convenient sequence.

The most economical approach to that objective appears to be to direct all the operator's signals, except one special "terminator" signal, into a buffer. The operator can put as long a string as he likes into the buffer. When he wants the signals to control action or to be acted upon, he presses the terminator key. The computer at once recognizes the terminator and calls a translator, a program that sorts the contents of the buffer into commands and data and puts them into a format determined in part by the syntax of the language and in part by the needs of the programs to be controlled or employed. The translator initiates the requested actions by executing the first command. From then on, processing follows the course determined by the commands in interaction with the program.

What is needed, we believe, is a synthesis of the good features of the several approaches that have been mentioned in the foregoing discussion. In order to control complex processes, an on-line interaction language must have a sophisticated syntax and a large vocabulary. At the same time, to cater to the user's convenience, it should minimize the requirement for complex or manifold control actions, and it should encourage the kind of convergence upon understanding achieved in conversation. To facilitate learning, and to promote efficient utilization of programs, on-line interaction languages should be compatible with one another and should fit together into a coherent system.

Representation language

The representation of information for storage and retrieval has already been discussed at length. Here we merely reiterate our conviction that both formalization and sophistication of language seem important for effective representation and efficient processing of a large corpus. We suspect that "the" representation language, if a single representation language ever becomes dominant over all its competitors, will be essentially a language system. It will have several sublanguages, specialized for different applications. Some of them may have as many syntactic categories as the natural languages and will distinguish among several thousand sharply defined semantic relations. Some of them may "understand" the complex interrelations among the semantic relations and the syntactic categories and deal competently with several dozen clearly defined information structures. Others will be simpler but less powerful.

We must distinguish between a language or sublanguage and its implementation through computer programming. One language or sublanguage may have several implementations, differing in compactness of packaging and speed of processing, but yielding the same answer to a given question and the same solution to a given problem. There will probably be a demand for two or more implementations of certain sublanguages in the procognitive system.

125

The over-all language will be a system because all the sublanguages will fall within the scope of one metalanguage. Knowing one sublanguage will make it easier to learn another. Some sublanguages will be subsets of others. There will be translators, as suggested earlier, to convert sets of data or domains of knowledge from one representation to another. One sublanguage will resonate with one discipline or problem, another with another. But the whole apparatus of representation will be internally consistent. It will be a coherent system — if the day ever arrives.

Meanwhile, every effort should be made to find a way out of the present chaos of fragmentary and incompatible schemes for representation. Standardization of terms and formats will doubtless help. The main hope, however, appears to lie in the development of community computing systems. The economic impracticality of having a different system for every user will force convergence. There will be an active market place and a strong incentive to form coalitions. Perhaps one coalition will become a monopoly. Monopoly should not be allowed to stifle research on languages and representations, but it should be encouraged to foster coherence within the operating system.

ADAPTIVE SELF-ORGANIZATION IN MAN-COMPUTER INTERACTION

In a sense, the whole of the procognitive system and its use is an adaptive, self-organizing process. The adaptive, self-organizing system includes, of course, the specialist personnel and the substantive users. One of the main goals to be sought through adaptive self-organization is recursive: it is increased effectiveness in growing, developing, adapting, and organizing. The other main goal, of course, is increased effectiveness in serving the substantive users.

Underlying the global aspect of adaptation and self-organization, there must be continual adaptation of the system to meet the needs of its users and a continuing development, on the part of the users, of the ability to take advantage of the services offered by the system and to improve the system in the process of using it.

We see the topic thus introduced as a very large and important one, but one that still remains almost unexplored. The prospects range all the way from simple adaptations that we know how to achieve, such as adjustment of the explicitness of user-oriented languages to the level of experience of the individual user, to regenerative self-organization of the procognitive system through its use by schools, colleges, and universities in education and in research. We have done enough work in computer-aided teaching and computer-facilitated study to sense that a procognitive system might contribute greatly to education by increasing the rewards to be won through intellectual effort. Let us end this section in a lower key, however. The console of the procognitive system will have two special buttons, a silver one labeled "Where am I?" and a gold one labeled "What should I do next?" Any time a user loses track of what he is doing, he can press the silver button, and the recapitulation program will help him regain his bearings. Any time he is at a total loss, he can press the gold one, and the instruction program will explain further how to use the system. Through either of those programs, the user can reach a human librarian.

EXPLORATIONS IN THE USE OF COMPUTERS IN LIBRARY AND PROCOGNITIVE FUNCTIONS

Part II introduces and summarizes briefly 13 elements of the program of exploration into uses of computers that constituted the major part of the two-year study. Chapter 5 is a survey of syntactic analysis by computer. Chapter 6 deals with quantitative aspects of files and text that bear upon the feasibility and efficiency of computer processing of library information. Chapter 7 describes a promising method for evaluating retrieval systems. Chapter 8 contrasts document-retrieval with fact-retrieval and question-answering systems. Chapter 9 describes eight efforts to develop, test, and evaluate computer programs that perform, or techniques that facilitate, library and procognitive functions.

CHAPTER FIVE

Syntactic Analysis of Natural Language by Computer

THE RELEVANCE of automated syntactic analysis to library procognitive systems lies in machine processing, and in eventual machine "understanding," of natural-language text. There is no thought that syntactic analysis alone — whether by man or machine — is sufficient to provide a useful approximation to understanding. On the other hand, there is no doubt that appreciation of the syntactic structure of natural-language text is a part, and an important part, of the over-all problem. Accordingly, Bobrow (1963) surveyed the work that has been done, and is being done, toward automation of syntactic analysis of English.

The efforts to automate syntactic analysis have been, essentially, efforts to implement various theories of grammar through the preparation of computer programs that

131

operate on natural-language text in the form of strings of encoded alphanumeric characters. The output of a successful syntactic-analysis program is one or more sets of assignments of the words of a sentence to grammatical categories ("parts of speech") plus, for each set of assignments, a representation of the grammatical structure of the sentence.

The grammars that have been used as bases for syntactic-analysis programs include dependency grammars, phrase-structure grammars with continuous and with discontinuous constituents, predictive grammars, string-transformation grammars, and phrase-structure transformational grammars. The main characteristics of, and differences among, these grammars are set forth in Bobrow's report. Although it is too early to say with assurance which of them is (or are) best for our purposes much expert intuition favors the phrase-structure, transformational approach.

Many of the programs that have been successful in making syntactic analyses have depended upon a distinction between "function words" and "content words." The distinction is a simple and familiar one. Function words are words such as "and," "or," "to," "from," "a," "an," "the," "neither," "nor," "if," and "whether." Content words are words such as "grammar," "equivalent," "structural," "diagram," "sentence," "minimum," "weekly," "accept," and "develop." There are, of course, many more types of content words than of function words. It is therefore reasonable to store in a computer memory very detailed descriptions of the functions, characteristics, idiomatic uses, and so forth, of the function words. The successful analytic programs have, in addition, employed dictionaries containing, for each content word, the grammatical categories into which it is normally expected to fall.

It is the intention here, not to give a complete summary of Bobrow's report, but rather to relate the idea of syntactic analysis by computer to the over-all picture set forth in Part I. Perhaps the best way to do that is to show in diagrammatic form some of the analyses that are described in detail by Bobrow.

The notion of "dependency" gives a direction and a hierarchical structure to syntactic relations. Adjectives depend on nouns, nouns depend on verbs and prepositions, adverbs and auxiliary verbs depend on main verbs, prepositions depend on the words modified by their phrases, and so forth. The system of dependency can be represented diagrammatically in the way illustrated for the sentences, "The man treats the boy and the girl in the park,"

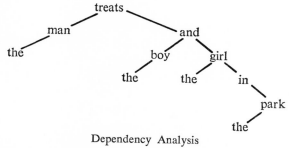

Dependency Analysis

and "The man at the door turned the light out."

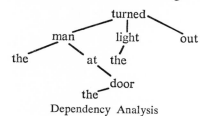

Dependency Analysis

133

This second sentence will be used to illustrate other grammars also, in order to display similarities and differences.

Computer programs capable of implementing dependency analysis have been developed or described by Hays (1962) of the RAND Corporation, by Kelly* of the RAND Corporation, by Gross (1962) of M.I.T., by Klein and Simmons (1963) of the System Development Corporation, and by several Russian workers, including Moloshnava (1960) and Andreyev (1962).

In a phrase-structure analysis that assumes continuous, immediate constituents,† the diagrammatic representation is again treelike, but the nodes of the branching structure are, at all levels except the lowest, syntactic or grammatical categories. At the lowest level, the actual words of the sentence appear. An immediate-constituent analysis of "The man ate the apple" is shown in the diagram.

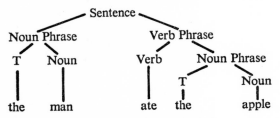

Immediate-Constituent Analysis

The analysis starts at the bottom of the diagram with the string of words and proceeds to discover a superstructure consistent with their grammatical class memberships. However, the analysis may involve trial-and-error differ-

---

* H. Kelly, Personal communication, September 1963.

† Immediate constituents are parts that are separated by the first step of an analysis, i.e., that are encountered immediately; they are to be contrasted with ultimate constituents. Continuous constituents are parts whose subparts are contiguous; continuous constituents are to be contrasted with discontinuous constituents.

entiation downward from assumed categories to strings of words.

The analysis substitutes for "Sentence" the two category names, "Noun Phrase" and "Verb Phrase." It then substitutes for "Noun Phrase" the category names "Definite Article" (or, since there is only one definite article in English, the symbol "T") and "Noun." For "Verb Phrase" it substitutes "Verb" and "Noun Phrase." It is then in a position to substitute actual words for three of the category names. "Noun Phrase," however, has to be passed through one more stage of analysis before the substitution of actual words can be made. The result of the analysis — the diagram — displays the roles of the individual words of the sentence and, in addition, shows how the several roles are interrelated.

The next diagram illustrates immediate-constituent

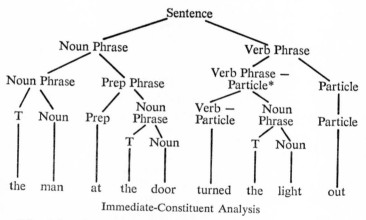

Immediate-Constituent Analysis

* Read the minus sign (not hyphen) as "minus."

analysis of "The man at the door turned the light out."

In the foregoing example, the analysis proceeded in a

135

succession of binary branchings. An alternative formulation makes use of multiple branching to produce coordinate structures with fewer levels. Bobrow compares binary structure and coordinate structure in the phrase, "the old black heavy stone."

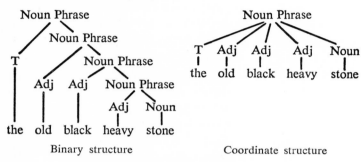

Binary structure   Coordinate structure

Immediate-Constituent Analysis

Computer programs capable of making immediate-constituent analyses have been developed or described by Robinson (1962) of the RAND Corporation, Cocke* of the International Business Machines Corporation, and Klein (1963) of the System Development Corporation.

Kuno and Oettinger of Harvard (1963) have developed extensively the technique of predictive analysis advocated by Rhodes (1961) of the National Bureau of Standards. Predictive analysis takes advantage of the fact that, once he has heard the beginning of a sentence, the listener can rule out many of the myriad syntactic patterns into which sentences are, a priori, capable of falling. Predictive analyses keep track only of the alternative interpretations that are consistent with the part of the sentence that has already been analyzed. At the very beginning, there are usually but few alternatives, for then

* John Cocke, Personal communication, September 1963.

136

the interpretations are not differentiated. In the mid-course of an analysis, there may be many possible ways in which the sentence can go. At the end, however, the analysis should converge upon one pattern of grammatical categories, or, at any rate, upon a set of patterns among which a choice can be made on the basis of semantic interpretation of the sentence itself and of its context. (Unfortunately for the prospects of machine "understanding," "context" must embrace both linguistic context and circumstantial or nonlinguistic context.) The Kuno-Oettinger programs determine all the alternatives. Related programs developed by Lindsay (1963) of the University of Texas find only one syntactic pattern but provide diagnostic information on the basis of which it is possible to clear up misinterpretation through "post-editing."

A minor problem for machine analysis is introduced by the fact that two words may together fill a grammatical category without being contiguous in text. This problem is not faced squarely by immediate-constituent grammars. In discontinuous-constituent grammars, however, the problem is recognized, and a special linkage is introduced to connect the separated parts. The diagram illustrates an analysis of "He called her up."

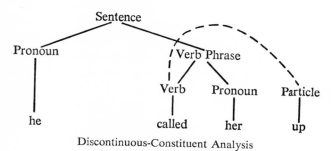

Discontinuous-Constituent Analysis

137

The linkage from "Verb" to "Particle" connects "up" to "called," from which it has been separated by "her." The diagram shows a discontinuous-constituent analysis of the standard sentence, "The man at the door turned the light out."

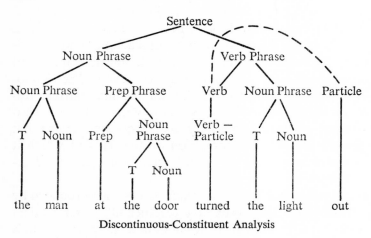

Discontinuous-Constituent Analysis

For the purposes of library procognitive systems, the most important problem in this subject area may well be one raised by Chomsky (1956, 1957). Chomsky was concerned that two expressions of the same idea, such as "The man drives the car" and "The car is driven by the man" do not have similar phrase structures and do not yield similar diagrams when analyzed in the ways we have been discussing. Chomsky handled this problem by setting up "transformation rules" that transform one sentence into another, or combine *n* sentences into one, or subdivide one sentence into *n* sentences. For example, one transformation takes a sentence from active voice to passive voice. Another transformation combines two single-clause sentences into a compound sentence. With transformation rules, one can build up complex syntactic structures from simple ones or analyze complex syntactic structures into simple ones. Bobrow gives an example in which the simple statements

1. X's are the airfields.
2. The airfields are in Ohio.
3. The airfields have runways.
4. The runways are long.
5. Two miles is long.

are derived from the question, "What are the airfields in Ohio having runways longer than two miles?" Analysis and synthesis based on such transformations will surely be important for machine-aided organization of the body of knowledge.

The transformational-grammar approach handles the discontinuous-constituent problem neatly. A transformation changes "turned the light out" into "turned out the light." As the diagram shows, the analysis then proceeds without any difficulty.

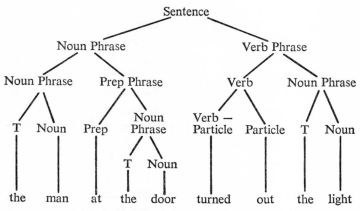

Intermediate Stage in Chomsky's Transformational Derivation

139

Walker and Bartlett (1962) of the Mitre Corporation are developing a parsing program based on a transformational grammar.

Harris (1962) and his associates at the University of Pennsylvania have developed a method of syntactic analysis that is intermediate between constituent analysis and transformational analysis. Although their method does not lend itself to representation by a tree diagram, a rough idea of its approach is conveyed by relating some of its terms to our standard sentence. In the sentence, the "string center" is ". . . man . . . turned out . . . light." One "the" is the "left adjunct" of "man," and the other is the "left adjunct" of "light." "At the door" is the "right adjunct" of "man." This "string-transformational grammar" has been implemented in the form of computer programs. The "Baseball" program developed by Green and associates (1961) at the Lincoln Laboratory — a program capable of answering questions about the outcomes of the baseball games played in the major leagues during one season — has a methodological kinship to the Pennsylvania work.

From Bobrow's survey, it is clear that automation of syntactic analysis is possible. Indeed, there are several operating syntactic-analysis programs. It is equally clear, however, that syntactic analysis is only a part — and perhaps, relatively, only a small part — of the over-all problem. The fact is that even the best analysis programs (excepting Lindsay's, which arbitrarily limits itself to a single syntactic pattern) produce discouragingly many alternative patterns. Selection among the alternatives has to be made on nonsyntactic grounds, and there has not been much progress toward automation of that selection. Furthermore, it is evident that one is a very long way from understanding what is being said when all he knows is the pattern or structure of syntactic categories into which the words of the message fit.

The question was raised in Part I, whether it is desirable, in formulating the basic concepts of this field, to separate syntactic and semantic factors into the two insulated bins of a rigid dichotomy, or whether, as subtler and subtler distinctions are made in the process now called syntactic analysis, that process will start to become semantic as well as syntactic. Although we are not in a position to decide, one way or the other, on that question, we have an intuitive feeling that the latter is more promising as a line of development. We should, in this connection, refer to work that we regard as extremely promising, work being carried out by F. B. Thompson and his colleagues (Thompson, 1963).

CHAPTER SIX

Research on Quantitative
Aspects of Files and Text

Two studies by Grignetti (1963*a*, 1964) deal with quantitative aspects of representations of information in digital memories. The first study concerns the average length of representations of descriptions of documents or, in greater generality, the average length of representations of "terms" (e.g., of descriptors associated with documents). The second concerns the informational measure "entropy" — or, to look at it the other way around, the redundancy — of English text considered as a string of words. Thus both studies bear upon the amount of memory required to store library information: the first with indexes, the second with actual text.

On the Length of a Class of Serial Files

From one point of view, the over-all organization and concept of a library or of a procognitive system is a more important thing to grasp, or to improve, than is the efficiency of a low-level "detail" function. On the other hand, a few functions that appear from one point of view to be mere details, to occupy low levels in the over-all system, are seen from another point of view to be both basic and ubiquitous. One of these functions that looks like a technical detail from one standpoint and like something very basic and general from another is the encoding of elements of information for storage in a digital memory. Let us, for the purposes of this discussion, adopt the point of view from which it seems important. As soon as we do that we may be prepared to examine subcategories, and one of the most conspicuous of these is the subcategory that includes catalogues and indexes. The study to be summarized deals with such files of information.

Perhaps the best schema to keep in mind while thinking about this problem is the schema of an index consisting of the names or numbers of the documents in a collection and, associated with each name or number, a list of terms or descriptors that characterize the corresponding document according to some coordinate indexing system. The problem under consideration is how to encode the terms. The object is to be economical in the use of storage space and, at the same time, to make it easy for a computer to decode the representation and determine the names or numbers (or addresses) of specified documents.

One of the most widely used techniques for representing terms is simply to spell them out in full or to record readable abbreviations of them. The direct way to encode such representations for storage in digital memory is to assign a binary code to each character in the character ensemble and to store the binary code patterns. That technique has the disadvantage of using much more memory space than is necessary. This kind of inefficiency is the subject of the study to be summarized in the next section.

A technique that is more economical of memory space is to number all the terms that may be used and to represent in memory in association with each item, not the corresponding terms themselves, but the numbers that were assigned to them. Since there are sometimes several terms per document, it is important not to let the numbers that represent different terms run together in such a way as to preclude subdivision of the over-all representation into its parts. The encodings of the sets of terms associated with different documents must also be kept separable. In the past, people have kept codes separable either by using special characters as separators or by adding enough leading zeros to the short codes to make all the codes the same length. (Fixing the length of the codes takes care only of separations within the set of terms associated with a given document, and not of separations between the sets of terms associated with different documents, but we may for the sake of simplicity limit our consideration to the problem of intraset separation.)

The prevailing opinion has been that the use of separators leads to more compact files than the use of fixed-length codes. The first thing Grignetti did was to analyze that comparison (1963a). It turned out that, on the average, and under certain reasonable assumptions, the fixed-length code is actually shorter than the variable-length code plus separator. If one thinks about this question with simple, schematic examples in mind, he is likely to doubt this conclusion of Grignetti's and to agree with the prevailing opinion that Grignetti finds incorrect. However, Grignetti's conclusion becomes quite obvious as soon as attention is focused upon large filing systems in which the list of legal terms is long. Consider, for example, that, of a list of nearly 1000 terms, almost 90 per cent would be represented by three-digit codes. About 9 per cent would require one leading zero, and about 1 per cent would require two leading zeros to bring them up to the "fixed" length of three digits.

In his work on coding efficiency, Grignetti also examined the notion that products of prime numbers might provide the basis for an effective coding system for the purpose we are considering here. In such a system, each term would be assigned a prime number, and the set of terms associated with a particular item would be represented by the product of the prime numbers associated with the members of the set. Grignetti was able to show conclusively that the prime-number code is an inefficient code, less good than either variant of the elementary system considered in the foregoing paragraphs.

The preliminary inquiries just described led Grignetti to look for a truly efficient coding system for terms (1964). He found one. He calls it the "combinational code." It is fairly easy to construct a combinational code. First, one has to decide the maximum number of terms that will be associated with an item, say, five. Second, he examines the list of legal terms, numbers the individual terms, and makes up all the possible combinations of term numbers, taken five or fewer at a time. Third, he orders the numbers corresponding to the terms of each combination (each set of five or fewer) in a sequence of

145

increasing magnitude. Fourth, he reorders the list of combinations according to a criterion that takes into account primarily the magnitude of the largest number in the subset but also, secondarily, the number of numbers in the subset. Finally, he assigns integers in increasing sequence to the members of the reordered list. Grignetti gives an analytical procedure for encoding and decoding. He points out that the procedure does not have to be changed, and that existing code numbers do not have to be altered, when new terms are added to the list of legal terms. Finally, he shows that the combinational code is the shortest possible code.

ENTROPY OF WORDS IN PRINTED ENGLISH

Grignetti's interest was attracted to the question of the representational efficiency of direct encodings of the strings of *words* that constitute text by the consideration, discussed in Part I, that storage of the body of knowledge in processible memories will be an important basis for procognitive systems (Grignetti, 1964). In order to estimate the representational efficiency, it is natural to compare determinations of the number of bits required to store a typical segment of text with estimates of the actual (Shannon-Wiener) information content of the text. The classical estimate of the information measure of a typical word of text is the one made by Shannon in 1951 on the assumption that the frequency of occurrence of word types is sufficiently approximated by Zipf's famous law. Shannon's estimate of the information measure, or entropy, was 11.82 bits per word. However, Bemer (1960), using roughly the approximation that Shannon used, calculated that words could be stored, on the average, in

10.76 bits of memory space — with the aid of a compression code that was obviously not optimal. That led Grignetti to examine Shannon's results closely.

By a method slightly different from Shannon's, a method that seems straightforward and in which no flaw has been detected, Grignetti found the information measure to be 9.7 or 9.8 bits per word.

From one point of view, the difference, which is only 2 bits per word, does not seem likely to have much practical significance. From another point of view, however, the important question is whether or not further work on encoding of text seems to be intellectually attractive. If it seems attractive, then it is possible, and perhaps likely, that a coding scheme will be found that is highly efficient in use of memory space and, at the same time, economical in respect of processing. On the other hand, if further work is not intellectually attractive, there is not likely to be an increase in either the efficiency of the use of space or the economy of encoding and decoding. Perhaps the 2 bits per word will have a stimulating effect. Clearly, the point on which study should now concentrate is the simplification of encoding and decoding.

CHAPTER SEVEN

A Measure of the Effectiveness of
Information-Retrieval Systems

To some information-retrieval systems, a particularly simple schema is appropriate. The system is a "black box" that contains a collection or set of items and that, from time to time, either spontaneously or in response to a request, offers a subset of its contents to one of its subscribers and withholds the complementary subset. An item may be thought of as a document. A subscriber may be thought of as simply a criterion: to the subscriber, an item is either pertinent or not pertinent. If one considers a single item of the collection and focuses his attention upon a particular occasion — a particular request from a subscriber or a particular spontaneous offering by the system — he sees that the performance of the system may be described simply by placing a tally mark in a two-by-two contingency table:

148

	P	$\overline{P}$
R		/
$\overline{R}$		

R means that the item was retrieved (offered); $\overline{R}$, not retrieved; P means that the item was pertinent (or would have proved pertinent if offered; $\overline{P}$, not pertinent. The tally mark indicates that the item in question was retrieved but did not meet the subscriber's criterion of pertinence.

It is natural to proceed from examination of the individual case to study of a large sample of cases. One then accumulates tally marks over the sample, counts the marks, and replaces them with numbers, i.e., with absolute frequencies or relative frequencies of occurrence. He can say, for example, that the system made a "hit" (retrieved a pertinent item) in 0.40 of the retrievals of individual items, a "miss" (withheld a pertinent item) in 0.20, a "false drop" (retrieved a nonpertinent item) in 0.10, and a "pass" (withheld a nonpertinent item) in 0.30. Note that only two of the relative frequencies are independent, for the sum over the four categories must be unity, and the fraction of the items that meets the subscriber's criterion of pertinence is assumed to be fixed. Note, also, that there has to be some way to ascertain the pertinence or nonpertinence of withheld items.

Investigating the problem of evaluation of effectiveness, Swets (1963) found that eight of the ten studies that met his criterion of pertinence reduced the analysis to two-by-two contingency tables. However, in none of the studies was advantage taken of the fact that evaluative procedures have been developed for, and found useful in, other fields of application (e.g., radar, sonar, psychophysics) in which performance may be summarized in two-by-two contingency tables. Swets therefore adapted some of the apparatus of statistical decision theory to the information-retrieval context and proposed a measure of merit, a measure that quantifies the ability of the system to maximize the expected value ("payoff") of a retrieval trial, i.e., of an offering or withholding of an individual item on a particular occasion. The measure takes into account the relative frequency and the utility (value minus cost) of each of the four categories in the two-by-two table. We shall not review here Swets's explanation of its derivation. Let it suffice to say that an assumption of normality of distribution is involved, that the measure is based on maximum-likelihood statistics, and that, given the relative frequencies of hits and false drops in a particular sample, one can read the value of the measure from an available table or graph.

The measure is simple, convenient, and appropriate. It gives definite meaning to the concept, the "basic discriminating power" of an information-retrieval system. The measure clearly separates discriminating power from mere willingness to yield output, thus avoiding a confusion that has been rife these last several years and that appears to be at the root of many informational difficulties. Moreover, the measure brings with it a well-developed system of procedures that facilitate analysis and interpretation of data.

We expect Swets's measure to prove useful in evaluation of information systems. The main obstacle may lie

150

in determination of the pertinence of withheld items. That obstacle is wide. It causes trouble for all the approaches to evaluation of performance in retrieval of information from large collections.

CHAPTER EIGHT

Libraries and
Question-Answering Systems

MARILL'S (1963) REPORT, "Libraries and Question-Answering Systems," laid the groundwork for subsequent research on question-answering systems. The report consists of three parts:

1. Two Concepts of a Library
2. Question-Answering Systems
3. Semantic Nets: Informal Introduction

The first of the "two concepts of a library" is a schematization of a present-day library. In the schema, the library consists of the collection of documents, the "tag" system (index, catalogue, terms, etc.), and the retrieval system that makes use of the tags to retrieve desired documents. The contributions that technology can make within this first concept are acceleration of document handling, automation of the process of "tagging" (assignment of terms to documents), and improvement of the retrieval process. Marill argues that this first concept, instrumented on a modest scale, would yield unsatisfactory results, and that, carried to its logical limit, it would be absurd.

The second concept of a library, according to Marill, is one in which the primary function is to provide not documents but information. The "system" of the second concept will be able to "read" and "comprehend" the documents themselves and not merely their tags. It will have a high capability for organizing the information internally.

It will be able to accept questions worded in natural English. If it has the requisite information available, it will answer the questions in natural English. Thus Marill advocates a very sophisticated procognitive system. He is concerned that people may believe the goal unreachable because it will be thought to require that inanimate mechanisms "think." Marill refers to the question-answering system called "Baseball" to forestall that misconception (Green et al., 1961).

In his discussion of question-answering systems, Marill defines the primary concepts: the corpus, the question, and the answer. The corpus consists of a set of quantificational schemata and their attendant predicate definitions, one definition for each predicate in the corpus. Thus Marill immediately seizes upon a predicate calculus as the formalism for representation of the information in the body of knowledge. There are two kinds of questions: questions satisfied by yes-no answers, and questions that require sentence answers.

Answers, therefore, are also of two types: yes-no answers and sentence answers. The answer to a yes-no question is "yes" if the question can be deduced from the corpus — if there exists a deduction that has the sentences of the corpus as premises and the question (in statement form) as the last line. The answer is "no" if the negation of the question can be deduced from the corpus. There is no answer (or the answer is, "I don't know,") if neither the question nor its negation can be deduced from the corpus. A sentence qualifies as a sentence answer if the sentence can be deduced from the corpus and if the schema of the sentence is the same as the schema of the question when the question is in statement form. There can be only one yes-no answer, but there can be any number of sentence answers.

Marill's treatment of semantic nets is an extension and formalization of the discussion of relational networks given in Part I. Marill takes the view that the proper structural analysis of a sentence is given by the quantificational schema of that sentence, as understood in symbolic logic. To this, he adds the view that the meaning of a one-place predicate is identified, ultimately, with the set of objects of which the predicate is true, and the meaning of a two-place predicate is identified with the set of all ordered pairs of objects of which the predicate is true, and so forth. Finally, he adds the notion that the meaning of an object is identified with, first, the set of one-place predicates that are true of the object, and, second, the set of two-place predicates that are true of it and something else, and so forth.

The sets (of predicates and objects) with which meanings are identified are extremely large. The machine cannot be required to prove its "understanding" of a meaning by producing all the members of the sets. Marill

154

maintains that it is enough for the machine to produce a convincingly large sample.

The usual representation of a quantificational schema has the form of a string of symbols. Marill views the semantic net as an alternative notation, equivalent to the string notation, but more promising for computer exploitation. To demonstrate the relation between semantic nets and string-form schemata, Marill starts with three simple statements in string notation and transmutes them, by degrees, into diagrams in which lines tie together the several instances of a variable.

The elements of a semantic net in Marill's exposition are the following.

1. Rectangles — which represent the truth functions corresponding to logical operators and their arguments. Each rectangle has one terminal for each argument.

2. Diamonds — which represent quantifiers. There are two types, corresponding to "some" and "all."

3. A triangle with point down — which represents "sentence." This triangle contains an "S."

4. A circle — which represents a predicate. The circle has as many terminals as there are places in the predicate.

5. A triangle with point up — which represents an individual.

Marill gives six rules governing the combination of elements and the formation of semantic nets. The rules are:

1. Connecting a predicate to a sentence symbol forms a sentence.

2. Inserting a negation rectangle between the sentence symbol and the predicate negates the sentence.

3. To connect two sentences, divert their predicates to

155

a two-place truth-function rectangle and connect it to a single sentence-symbol triangle.

4. To add a quantifier to a sentence, insert it in the line between the sentence symbol and its nearest neighbor.

5. To terminate an unterminated predicate, attach an individual object to the unused terminal, or connect that terminal to a quantifier that is already in the diagram of the sentence.

6. To merge two or more networks into one: (step 1) for each individual, overlay all the triangles that represent the individual, retaining all the lines that are attached to any of the triangles; (step 2) associate all the occurrences of the same predicate by connecting them with "association lines."

In "Semantic Nets: An Informal Introduction," Marill presents diagrams to illustrate the rules and to demonstrate the interpretation of moderately complex semantic nets. Marill's diagrams and discussion make it clear that the semantic net is formally equivalent to the conventional representation of a system of statements in predicate calculus. Marill believes that semantic nets afford a promising path into computer representation and processing of complex systems of relations.

CHAPTER NINE

Studies of Computer
Techniques and Procedures

THE FOLLOWING EIGHT STUDIES are concerned with early steps along the course from present digital-computer system to future procognitive systems. Let us consider the studies in the order of their locations along that course. The first ones were intended merely to make it convenient to carry out some of the functions that are required in research on library and procognitive problems or in the efficient use of large collections of documents. The last ones in the sequence were intended to explore functions that we think will actually be involved in future procognitive systems.

An "Executive" Program to Facilitate the Use of the PDP-1 Computer

One of the first needs of the study was a computer program to facilitate the programming and use of the laboratory's digital computer. The computer is a small but excellent machine, Digital Equipment Corporation PDP-1, specialized to facilitate interaction with users who work "on line." The PDP-1 has an oscilloscope display with light pen, several electric typewriters, a set of programmable relays, an analogue-to-digital converter, and an assortment of switches and buttons. Its primary memory is small (8196 eighteen-bit words), but it is capable of transferring information rapidly between the primary memory and a secondary drum memory that holds about 90,000 eighteen-bit words. Associated with the computer are two magnetic-tape units. With the computer, it is possible to implement, in a preliminary and schematic way, several of the functions that were described in Part I as functions desirable in a procognitive system.

One encounters two main difficulties in trying to do, with the PDP-1 computer, research oriented toward a future period in which information-processing machines will have more advanced capabilities. First, although the machine is reasonably fast (5-microsecond memory cycle), and although its secondary and tertiary memories make it possible to work with significantly large bodies of information, the machine is not capable of performing deep and complicated operations on really large bodies of text with the speed that would be desired in an operational system. The result is that it may take 30 seconds or a minute to get something that one would like to have

158

almost instantly, that the display flickers on the oscillo-scope screen, and so forth. Second, there is not available, at present, on any machine, either a programming language or a man-machine interaction (user-oriented) language that makes it easy to do, or possible to do rapidly, many of the things envisioned in the discussion of procognitive systems in Part I of this report. Our approach, during the study, was simply to put up with, and make allowances for, the shortcomings of the hardware system. It was easy to do that in informal experiments conducted by members of the research group; it was not realistic, however, to hope that all the observers of demonstrations would make the necessary allowances, and the shortcomings of the equipment (compared to what we expect to have in two decades) effectively precluded formal experimentation. Nevertheless, the equipment situation was at least tolerable, in terms of absolute assessment, and it seemed superb when we compared our man-computer interaction situation with any but two or three of all the others with which we were acquainted.

The unavailability of highly developed languages — and, of course, the interpreter and compiler programs that would be required to make them useful — was, however, a seriously inhibiting factor. During the period of our study, two good programming-language systems came into being: DECAL, which is a quite elegant and powerful language and compiler of the ALGOL type, suitable for a small computer, and MACRO, which is an ingenious language and assembler system that incorporates several of the features that DECAL lacks and lacks several of the features that DECAL incorporates. However, neither DECAL nor MACRO was designed for on-line programming, and neither was designed particularly to handle the problems that seem likely to present themselves to users of procognitive systems.

Those considerations led to the effort, which was never quite completed, to develop a composite programmer-oriented and user-oriented system to facilitate our research in man-machine interaction. The system is called "Exec," which stands, of course, for "executive program" and thus expresses something about the mode of operation: statements of the input language, coming into the computer, are examined by the executive program, and, depending upon whether or not they fall into the class requiring interpretation, are either interpreted and executed with the aid of a set of subroutines associated with the executive program or simply executed as machine instructions.

Exec was written originally in the symbolic language called "FRAP" and had, as its main function, simplification of the preparation of programs and subroutines to be translated and assembled by FRAP. When DECAL became available, Exec was rewritten in DECAL, and slight modifications were made to facilitate the use of Exec in the preparation of programs and subroutines to be translated and compiled by DECAL. The original intention — to develop Exec to the point at which it could operate as an on-line language as well as an adjunct to a programming language — was not accomplished.

One of the main themes in the work on Exec was to simplify and regularize the "calling" and "returning" of subroutines. In most computer-programming systems, and especially in the computer-programming systems that will be required in the implementation of plans of the kind described in Part I, a computer program is a complex arrangement of parts. The highest echelon of the structure does little more than represent the chapter headings of the general plan. The actual work — the detailed processing of data — is handled by subprograms or "subroutines" that break the task down into successively simpler subpackages at successively lower levels of detail until, finally, there is nothing left for the lowest-echelon subprograms to do but to perform simple, explicitly defined operations upon the few codes or numbers that are supplied to them. In this process of successive delegation of responsibility, the transactions that appear repeatedly are the "calling" of a lower-echelon subroutine by a higher-echelon subroutine and the "returning" of control from the lower-echelon subroutine to the higher-echelon subroutine. Calling usually includes transmission of instructions, and also the designation of the arguments upon which the lower-echelon subroutine must operate, from the calling subroutine to the called subroutine. The transmission of information down the line we shall call "briefing." Transmission of results up the line we shall call "debriefing."

In the conventional way of handling calling and returning, a subroutine eventually returns control to the subroutine that called it, but it may first call one or more lower-echelon subroutines.

Fortunately or unfortunately, depending upon one's point of view, there are many different ways in which subroutines can be called and briefed and in which they can return control and do their debriefing. As indicated, one of the main purposes of Exec is to simplify and regularize this whole process.

In order to simplify the process of calling and returning, Exec is interposed between the calling subroutine and the called subroutine at the time of calling and between the called (and now returning) subroutine and the calling (and now receiving) subroutine at the time of returning. With each subroutine is associated a compact code, that provides Exec with a description of the needs of the subroutine. Exec can therefore handle in a systematic, centralized manner several of the functions that would otherwise have to be handled by each subroutine. In taking a burden off the routines, Exec takes a burden off the programmers who prepare them.

The arrangements in Exec for calling and returning are set up in such a way that the chain of subroutine calls can be recursive. That is to say, it is possible for subroutine *A* to call subroutine *A*, or for subroutine *A* to call a subroutine *B* which, directly or through one of its minions, called subroutine *A*. To permit recursive operation, one must handle "temporary storage" — storage of the scratch-pad jottings made by each subroutine during its operation — in such a way that results written by *B*, for example, do not destroy results that *A* calculated before calling *B* and will need to use after *B* returns control.

The functions just described have been implemented in a few programming systems — notably in the systems called IPL and LISP. In IPL and LISP, however, one either works wholly within the system or does not use the system at all. Exec extends the basic programming language (DECAL) and provides the new capabilities and conveniences within the structure of DECAL.

In implementing the handling of subroutines, we made use of the technique of the "pushdown list." A pushdown list (or "stack") is an arrangement for storing information that resembles the spring-supported tray on which

162

plates are stored in restaurants. If one puts a plate (computer word) onto the top of the stack, it pushes all the others down, and if one then takes the plate (word) off the top, the others pop up again. Exec, itself, employs one pushdown list. Another pushdown list is available to the programmer or user through simple commands. He has only to give the name of the entity to be stored into the pushdown list or returned from it and to say whether he wants to push it down or pop it up. In the process of handling a call to a subroutine or a return from a subroutine, Exec examines the subroutine's heading code, determines whether or not, and how, to fulfill each of a number of functions, and then carries out those required. These functions include protecting contents of certain special registers of the processor against destruction during the running of the subroutine, finding the arguments needed by the subroutine and displaying them for its use, accepting the results obtained by the subroutine and communicating them to the calling routine, and protecting the contents of various temporary storage registers and "flag" registers against modification by the called subroutine. Exec protects information by putting it into the pushdown list.

A second general purpose of Exec is to provide the advantages of generality and the advantages of specificity, both at the same time and within the same system. If a computer program is written in such a way as to make it useful in a particular situation — for example, to make it operate on words and not sentences, and on the contents of Table 3 instead of the contents of Table 4 — then a new program must be written every time the specifics of the problem change. On the other hand, if the program is written so that for example, it alphabetizes or orders any kind of strings of alphanumeric text in any file or table, then, when the programmer starts to use it on the words listed in Table 3, he has to communicate to it, or have the routine that calls it communicate to it, that it should operate on words and on Table 3, and that it should alphabetize according to a specified alphabet.

In Exec, an effort is made to accommodate very general subroutines and to make it maximally convenient to communicate to them the information required to prepare them for specific applications. This is done by setting up and maintaining a description of the prevailing context of operation. In the terms of the example, his description may contain a specification that the currently prevailing string class is the class of "words." It contains the specification that the x, in any subroutine prepared to operate upon "Table x," should be interpreted as 3. The subroutine, therefore, automatically performs on Table 3 the operation intended by the programmer, despite the fact that the programmer was thinking in terms of abstractions and not in terms of the particular present task. (Exec makes it possible to write subroutines in terms of table variables x, y, and z simultaneously. A sequence of sentences can, for example, be taken out of Table x, and the odd-numbered ones can be stored in Table y and the even-numbered ones in Table z. The values of x, y, and z can be set later to 17, 4, and 11, respectively.)

With arrangements of the kind just suggested, Exec makes it possible to use a subroutine that contains the expression, "next string," for example, to operate on the next character, or the next word, or the next sentence, or the next paragraph, or the next section, or the next chapter, and so forth. Exec keeps track of three "string classes" simultaneously, class u, class v, and class w. At any time, the programmer can set any one of the string classes to any one of seven levels. He can write, for example, "sscu word," meaning to *set* the *s*tring *c*lass *u* to have the value, *word*. From that time on, until the instruction is superseded, all the subroutines that deal with the string class hierarchy *u* will consider the *u* strings to be words.

The procedure for designating tables is similar to that for designating strings. If the programmer would like to have programs written in terms of Tables x, y, and z operate on the contents of Table zones 2, 5, and 7, he writes "ntox 2, ntoy 5, ntoz 7." * When Exec sees those instructions, it does more than merely substitute 2 for x, 5 for y, and 7 for z. It finds the descriptions, in its file of table descriptions, that characterize the three numbered tables, and it substitutes these descriptions for the pre-previously prevailing descriptions of Tables x, y, and z, respectively. When a subroutine operates on the contents of the table, it examines the table's description and controls its processing accordingly.

This makes it possible to accommodate diverse formats and conventions. Inasmuch as the adjustments are made "interpretively" during the running of the program, the user can change his mind and reprocess something in a slightly different way without having to go through extensive revision and recompilation of his programs. This is an advantage that the present technique has over the technique, based on the "communication pool," that has been developed in connection with the programming of very large computer systems — systems programmed by teams so large as to discourage the effort to enforce the

---

* The italics are introduced here in the hope of bringing out the mnemonic significance of the code: "move n to x, and let n be 2." The programmer's typewriter does not have italic type.

165

use of a single, standard set of conventions and formats. The part of Exec that we have been describing is approximately an interpretive communication pool.

The third set of functions with which Exec is concerned has to do with the display of alphanumeric information on typewriters and on the oscilloscope screen. Although these are very simple functions, they involve enough detailed programming to be a nuisance unless they are handled in a systematic way. Exec makes it convenient to separate specification of the information to be displayed from specification of the equipment through which it is to be displayed. It uses standard programs to handle strings that are long enough to be considered messages or texts, but it provides special arrangements to facilitate preparation of labels, headings, and the like. For example, the programmer can call for the typing of any particular character x on whatever typewriter is currently specified to be typewriter b simply by writing "typ$b$ x." If the programmer wants the character to appear upon the screen of oscilloscope a (there is only one oscilloscope now, but we hope to have more), he writes "scp$a$ x." With the aid of Exec, the programmer can define in equally short instructions the size of the print, the vertical position at which the text should begin, and other parameters of the visual display. Exec's arrangements for displaying capital and lower-case letters on the oscilloscope are primitive, but it is a step in the right direction to have both capital and lower-case letters. At present, a "lower-case" letter is simply a small capital letter. We settled for that stop-gap solution only in the interest of economy.

The fourth and final set of functions handled by Exec has to do with display, by the computer, of what the computer is doing. One technique developed for this purpose, a technique called "Introspection," will be described in a later section because it was developed as a separate project. The arrangements described here are integral to Exec.

One of the main causes of difficulty in man-computer interaction is that the computer does not give the man any good clues about what it is doing until it completes a segment of processing and spews forth the results. When the computer is running, its lights flash so fast that they are scarcely interpretable. It seems important to provide a way of having the computer give a running account of its processing.

A part of Exec called the "Reporting Subsection" — an optional part — is brought into play each time a subroutine is called and each time a subroutine returns control to its caller. When the reporting subsection is brought into action, it examines the list of things that it should do. This list can be changed while Exec and other programs are running. Ordinarily, the first thing on the list is to give the address, and, if it is available in the directory, also the name, of the subroutine that is being called or that is returning control to its caller. Since the subroutines operate very rapidly, the names and addresses would appear to be presented simultaneously, one on top of another, if they were shown in a fixed location on the screen. Therefore they are displayed in a format corresponding to that of a conventional outline. If a chain of subroutines is called, each one operating at a level just lower than its caller, the names and addresses appear on successive lines of the display with increasing indentation. Then, as the subroutines return control, each to its caller, the names and addresses are displayed again in such a way as to redisplay the outline pattern from bottom to top.

167

To the display just described can be added, at the option of the operator, a display of the contents of the active registers of the computer. In addition, the operator may see the contents of whatever parts of the computer's memory he wants to examine. He designates the various parts of memory to Exec by typing on the typewriter while the program is running. He can change his prescription at will. He may, for example, ask to see the contents of Table x, the contents of Table 3, and the program of the subroutine itself. The current version of Exec allows him to specify nine different sectors of memory, either symbolically or in terms of absolute addresses. When he indicates that he wants to see "the subroutine," Exec interprets "the subroutine" to mean the particular subroutine that is being called, or that is returning control to its caller. That will, of course, be one subroutine at one moment and another at another moment. When the operator wishes to examine a table or a program in detail, he touches the space bar of the typewriter. That causes the system to pause in its progression through the sequence of things to be displayed, and to hold the current display until the operator releases it by touching the tab key.

The Reporting Subsection provides a few additional conveniences — minor ones introduced from time to time on an *ad hoc* basis — but the foregoing will suffice to give an idea of the existing arrangement. Let us mention a few of the steps not yet accomplished, however. It seems worth while to connect to the Reporting Subsection the "Introspection" programs that will be described later. It is necessary to complete the arrangements that associate the tables $(x, y, z, 1, 2, 3, \cdot \cdot \cdot)$ that reside in the primary memory to corresponding structures in secondary and tertiary memory and, in the manner of the Atlas computer system, to arrange it so that information structures are automatically shifted up through the memory hierarchy whenever they are addressed. It is necessary, also, to expand the mechanism that associates symbols with machine addresses. That mechanism is only a simple table-searching system, but it is inherently capable of effecting the translation required to make conveniently readable the reports of "what is currently going on in the computer."

We found it useful to distinguish, in Exec, between "intrinsic" and "extrinsic" subroutines. Exec is highly "subroutinized" and has the partly hierarchical, partly recursive, structure that we have described as essential for procognitive systems. Each subfunction of Exec that appears to have any likelihood of proving useful in future applications is separated out and set into the form of a subroutine.

In the process of writing subroutines to handle substantive problems — subroutines that made use of Exec but were not at first intended to be part of the Exec system — we encountered repeatedly several sets or clusters of functions. By associating with Exec the subroutines prepared to handle those functions, we were able to build up a system of considerable convenience and power. The part of the system not intrinsic to Exec was too extensive to be held in primary memory at all times. However, it was clearly desirable to bring parts of it into primary memory — coherent clusters of it corresponding to major functions — whenever required in the execution of a program.

The easiest way to accomplish dynamic storage and transfer of subroutines, and to handle the associated bookkeeping, was to take care of it automatically through Exec's ability to examine calling sequences and subroutine headings. We did not make much progress toward that end during the course of the study. However, we did work with the problem enough to see the great convenience and power that reside in a coherent structure of computer subroutines and a largely automatic arrangement for calling them and transferring information among them. Evidently, the more sophisticated the arrangements, the larger the fraction of the subroutines that will be intrinsic to the arrangements. We visualize a system in a continual process of development, with a set of intrinsic subroutines, a set of extrinsic subroutines, and a continual flow from the extrinsic set to the intrinsic set as more and more functions are brought within the scope and capability of the system.

ON-LINE MAN-COMPUTER COMMUNICATION

"On-Line Man-Computer Communication" by Licklider and Clark (1962) discusses several problems in, and several steps toward the improvement of, interaction of men and computers. These include problems and developments in the use of computers as aids in teaching and in learning and as a basis for group cooperation in the planning and design of buildings. The part of the paper that stemmed from the present study was the development of a pair of programs, referred to earlier as "Introspection," that are closely connected with the last-described major function of Exec.

The two programs of "Introspection" were designed to demonstrate that, although present-day computers are opaque and inscrutable, of all the complex organisms and systems in the world, computers are, in principle, the most capable of revealing the intricacies of their internal processes. We consider this to be an important problem calling for much research. Our two programs constitute only exploratory steps.

The two parts of Introspection are "Program Graph" and "Memory Course." Program Graph displays, in the form of a graph relating that quantity to time, the contents of any specified register or registers of the computer. Memory Course displays the progression of control from one memory register to the next during the operation of a program. With the aid of these two programs, the operator can see what is happening, as it happens, within the processor and the memory of the computer. These programs give him at once both a global view and a considerable amount of detail. They let him see relations among parts of the over-all picture. No longer is he constrained, as he has been with conventional procedures, to peek at the contents of one register at a time, and to build up the over-all picture from myriad examinations of microscopic details.

To provide a rough impression of the operation of Program Graph, it may suffice to describe how it operates when it is set to display the contents of the register of the computer that is called the "program counter." The program counter contains the address of the memory register that contains the instruction that is being executed. In the absence of "branching" or "jumping," control proceeds from one register to the next, and the contents of the program counter increase by one, each time an instruction is executed. When a "branch" or "jump" occurs, the number in the program counter changes by some integral quantity different from one, and often the

171

increment or decrement is rather large. Program Graph plots the graph relating the number in the program counter to the time. The display presents about a thousand individual quantities simultaneously to view. From the graph, it is easy to recognize the upward-sloping line segments that correspond to nonbranching, nonjumping stretches of program. When the program "loops," as it often does, branching backward and repeating a sequence of instructions over and over, the display shows a sawtoothed waveform. When the program calls a subroutine, the jump to the subroutine, the loops within the subroutine, and the return from the subroutine are all clearly evident.

When Program Graph is used to display the contents of the accumulator, the input-output register, or one of the memory registers, the interpretation of the graph is, of course, quite different. In general, however, its main value lies in its presentation of a large quantity of information in such a way that relations among parts are easy to perceive.

The other Introspection program, Memory Course, displays only the course through memory followed by the program under study. It shows that course as a succession of circles connected by a heavy line against a gridlike background representing the primary memory of the computer. The grid upon which the display of Memory Course is shown consists of 4096 dots, arranged in 64 squares of 64 dots each, and representing one bank of memory. A register is represented by a very fine light dot if the instruction and the address it contains are both zero. The dot is a little heavier if the instruction is not zero. The dot is a little heavier still if the address is not zero. If both the instruction and the address are

172

not zero, the dot is heavy. From the grid, therefore, the user can see which parts of memory are occupied and which are not. In addition, after he has gotten used to the display, he can make out which parts of memory are used to store programs, and which parts are used to store data.

When Memory Course is used to display the "trajectory" through memory followed by an object program, the object program itself is not run in the usual way. Instead, the object program is operated by Memory Course, which "traces" the progress of the object program and displays it on the oscilloscope screen. Each time an instruction is executed, a circle is drawn around the dot that corresponds to the location of the instruction in the computer memory. When a program "loop" is traced, the line is set over slightly to one side of the circles it has been connecting. That keeps it from retracing its path backwards and helps it represents the cyclic nature of the course.

Memory Course represents loops, as just suggested, by tracing out a closed course. When the program transfers control to a subroutine, a line jumps out from the dot that corresponds to the call and leads to the dot that corresponds to the beginning of the subroutine. Thus, Memory Course provides a simple, maplike representation of the program structure. One can see where the various subroutines are, how long they operate, when they receive their calls, and when they return control to their callers. If an error occurs, either in the computer or in the program, control is very likely to be transferred to an inappropriate location. If the user knows the structure of his program, either from having programmed it or from experience operating it, he sees that something unexpected has happened. He then looks back to the beginning of the unexpected line and determines precisely the location of the register within which the error originated. Having done that, he typically reruns the program, following its course very carefully as it approaches the critical point. If the error recurs, he reruns the program once more, this time stopping it at various points ahead of the critical one and using other means to examine the instructions, addresses, and data associated with those points.

A File Inverter

The project to be described next was aimed, like Exec, at increasing the convenience and effectiveness with which the computer could be used in the study of library and procognitive problems. This project, however, had a much sharper focus than Exec. Its aim was simply to implement the operation called "file inversion."

A direct file is ordered with respect to its "items," and usually several terms are associated with each item. An inverse file is ordered with respect to its "terms," with several items usually associated with each term. Obviously, both the direct file and the inverse file are aspects of a more general structure consisting of items, terms, and associations between items and terms.

The "File Inverter" is a computer program, written in DECAL by Grignetti (1963b), that accepts a direct file and produces an inverse file. Since there is no difference in abstract format between a direct file and an inverse file, the program produces a direct file if it is presented with an inverse one.

The file-inverting program includes a subprogram that

174

alphabetizes the entries. If it is used to invert a file consisting of terms associated with alphabetized items, it yields a file of items associated with alphabetized terms. If the items consist of the bibliographic citations of documents, and if the terms are the key words of the titles of the documents, then the result obtained by applying the file-inverting program is a kind of "permuted title index." Grignetti's program includes a subprogram that facilitates the selection of key words from titles (or from abstracts or from texts). The subprogram selects from a string of words all those that do not appear upon a list of words to be excluded. The list of words to be excluded ordinarily contains the "function" words and, also, words that have been found not to discriminate.

An Automated Card Catalogue

Using parts of the file-inverting program, Grignetti (1963b) prepared a program that automates some of the functions involved in using an ordinary card index. The kind of card index toward which the program is oriented is not precisely the kind used in most libraries. It differs mainly in assuming that each card will contain a series of descriptive terms. Such card indexes are found more frequently in documentation centers that specialize in laboratory technical reports and reprints than in libraries of books and serials.

The "Automated Card Catalogue" is a DECAL program for use in exploration of card catalogue problems. The user sits at the computer typewriter and presents his retrieval prescription to the computer in the form of a Boolean function of the terms in which he is interested. A person interested in non-digital simulations of neural processes, particularly including studies made under the heading, "perceptron," but also other studies in the field of artificial intelligence, might type:

```
(artificial inteligence or perceptron or
neural simulation) and not digital
```

Using the terms of the Boolean function as retrieval terms, the program searches a magnetic tape containing the "card" file. Whenever it finds one of the terms, it looks further within the entry to determine whether or not the function is satisfied. If the function is satisfied, the program displays the entire contents of the "card" on the oscilloscope screen for examination by the user.

Grignetti's program makes it convenient for the user to correct his retrieval prescription, to reinitiate a search, to find out just where he stands at any point in his study, and to save "cards" for future reference. The program "knows" the rules for regular pluralization and considers the search for a term to be satisfied if either the singular or a calculated regular plural or a given irregular plural of the term is found. In addition, the program works with a simplified system of spelling, as well as with literal spelling, and is therefore often able to find the desired term on a "card" even when the term is misspelled in the prescription. In such an instance, it displays, for example,

Do you mean "intelligence"?

The user then types y for "yes" or n for "no." The program remembers this answer and does not bother the user again with the same question. That may be convenient when the user is dealing with names he does not know very well, but it leads to complications that will have to be settled through further programming. Probably it will be better to correct the prescription than to perpetuate the indiscrimination.

A SYSTEM TO FACILITATE THE STUDY OF DOCUMENTS

The two programs described in the preceding sections are related to, and are intended for incorporation into, a system to facilitate the retrieval and study of documents. The "study" part of the over-all system is described in a report by Bobrow, Kain, Raphael, and Licklider (1963).

The study system, called "Symbiont" because we hope to develop it into a truly symbiotic partner of the student, displays information to the student via the typewriter or the display screen. It is intended as an exploratory tool, for use mainly by students who are at the same time experimenters, and it does not yet have the perfection or polish required for realistic demonstration or practical application. However, it does make available, in a single, integrated package, several functions that prove quite useful to a student who wants to examine a set of technical documents, take notes on their contents, compare or combine graphs found in different papers, and so forth.

Among the functions provided by Symbiont are the following:

1. Present for examination a document specified by any sufficiently prescriptive segment of its bibliographic citation.

2. Turn pages, forward or backward, in response to the pressing of a key.

3. Permit designation of a passage (segment of text)

by pointing to the beginning and then the end with a light pen.

4. Accept labels from the typewriter and associate them with passages of text.

5. Record as a note, and preserve for later inspection, any designated passage.

6. Append bibliographic citations to extracted passages.

7. Accept retrieval prescriptions from the typewriter.

8. Accept from the typewriter coded versions of specifications of such operating characteristics as, "Consider a neighborhood to be five consecutive lines of text," or "Consider a search to be satisfied when any two of the three elements of the search have been satisfied."

9. Carry out retrieval searches and display passages in which the retrieval prescriptions are satisfied.

10. Compose graphs from tabulated data and present the graphs, against labeled coordinate grids, on the oscilloscope screen.

11. Set two graphs side by side to facilitate comparison.

12. Expand or compress the scales of graphs, under control from the light pen.

13. Change the number of grid lines or the calibration numbers associated with the lines, or both together, and recalculate and redisplay the calibration numbers when grid lines are added or deleted.

The search routines used in finding desired passages of text operate with three sets of retrieval terms. The user specifies the terms of each set initially through the typewriter. All the terms of a subset are considered equivalent during the search, and the search is satisfied insofar as that subset is concerned if any one of the terms is encountered in the text. The user can specify whether he wants to find a passage in which at least one of the terms of one of the sets occurs, or a passage in which at least one of the terms of each of two of the sets occurs, and so forth. Even though this implementation is primitive, it is evident from preliminary experiments with Symbiont that automation of the function of searching for "ideas" will be a very powerful aid in technical study. Machine aid in manipulating graphs will also be very helpful.

ASSOCIATIVE CHAINING AS AN INFORMATION-RETRIEVAL TECHNIQUE

Most of the information-retrieval systems that have actually been developed, and even most of those that have been subjected to intensive research, retrieve unitary elements of information, such as documents, paragraphs, or sentences. A basic point in Marill's (1963) paper, discussed in Chapter 8, is that for many purposes the retrieval of a unitary part of the corpus is inadequate, and that what often is needed is an answer to a question that may have to be derived through deduction from elements of information scattered throughout the corpus. The associative chaining technique to be described briefly in this section is a step in Marill's direction. It does not go as far as the techniques described in the final two sections, but it does go beyond the single, unitary element of the corpus to explore "chains" of relation between one element of the corpus and another. When the relation between two items is direct, they are said to be connected by a first-order chain. When the relation between two

179

items can be established only through the intermediary agency of a third item, the first two items are said to be connected by a chain of second order, and so forth.

In a report on "Associative Chaining as an Information Retrieval Technique," Clapp (1963) describes the idea of chaining as a general schema, then shows the correspondence between the chaining schema and certain schemata of graph theory, and finally discusses a program that traces chains of relevance through corpora consisting of files of sentences.

Chaining, as a technique, is particularly simple and easy to discuss when it is separated from the problem of the nature of relevance. In Clapp's work, the two things — the technique and the concept of relevance — are well separated. For purposes of simplicity and convenience, Clapp considers two sentences to be directly associated if they have one or more words in common. Thus, the sentences, "The cat is black," and "Black is a color," are directly associated. They have two words in common, "is" and "black." There is no direct, first-order association between the first two of the following sentences, but only a second-order association through the third sentence: "The cat is black," "Feline animals move gracefully," "A cat is a feline animal." It is obvious, even at the outset, that something has to be done to inhibit associations based on the common occurrence of frequently used verbs and function words. In Clapp's approach, however, whatever is done about that is a separate matter from the development of the algorithm that traces out the chains.

Clapp's computer programs are divided into two sets. The first set of programs facilitates the preparation of a machine-processible file of information units, such as sentences, paragraphs, or documents. It then prepares, from the file, a series of concordances. Finally, with the aid of the concordances, it determines the set of all first-order associations. The second set of programs operates upon a retrieval prescription plus the set of first-order associations. The retrieval prescription is a set of words drawn from the vocabulary of the corpus. The first thing that the chaining algorithm does is to find all those elements of the corpus that contain all the words of the prescription. This is what a "conventional" information-retrieval system would do. Then, however, the chaining algorithm goes on to trace higher-ordered chains through the corpus and to retrieve the information elements that are involved in higher-ordered chains up to some cutoff order specified by the operator.

The program has been tested and demonstrated only with a corpus consisting of sentences. Except for minor considerations having to do with delimiters — the clues that mark stopping points such as ends of sentences or paragraphs — the chaining programs are not sensitive to the distinctions among sentence, paragraph, document, and so forth, and it is obvious that the chaining operation can be carried out on textual strings of any class. However, pursuing the technique of chaining based on the common occurrence of words beyond a level of the sentence does not seem to offer much promise. It is evident that every book would be directly associated with almost every other book if the criterion were a word in common, and it is equally evident that almost no book would be associated with any other book if the criterion were a verbatim paragraph in common. For the technique of chaining, ordinary sentences seem to be approximately the optimal length.

Fortunately, the sets of descriptive terms used in coordinate-indexing systems are of approximately the same length as sentences. The notion of association based on inclusion of common terms is quite appropriate for them. It is in that domain that we think it most likely that the chaining technique, and the chaining algorithms developed by Clapp, will find practical application.

In his exploration of the relations between graph theory and associative chaining, Clapp developed the chaining schema in considerably more depth than is reflected in this summary. For example, his development uses the number of parallel links as well as the order of the links in the chain of association. Some of his ideas (but not the algorithms thus far programmed) recognize gradations in the strength of association. That seems important because, intuitively, one thinks of relevance as capable of variation in degree.

The next step in the development of the concept of associative chaining, we think, should be an attempt to define the fundamental relatedness or relevance on which the "association" is based. Associative chaining has a natural connection with the relational networks described in Part I and with the semantic nets and question-answering systems studied by Marill and Black. The next step may, therefore, take the form of merging the chaining concept with the concepts underlying the relational and semantic nets and the question-answering systems.

Two Question-Answering Systems

Marill's (1963) short paper on question-answering systems, described earlier, initiated a series of studies that involved a meld of symbolic logic and computer programming. Most of these studies were carried out by

Black, who described them in a series of memoranda and a report (1963). The memoranda and the report share with the corpora of the question-answering systems a tight, terse, logical quality that makes them attractive to the logician and difficult for the nonlogician to understand. Following is an effort to summarize, without gross distortion, two of the principal accomplishments of the work on question-answering systems in a freer and less formal exposition. One might justify this aim by quoting a paragraph from Black's "Conclusions on QAS," a memorandum dated November 13, 1963:

A string of words cannot be rephrased without significant loss of facts or ideas relevant to some area. However, if we limit ourselves to certain areas, then the string of words can be rephrased without loss of facts or ideas *relative to those areas.*

In the final paragraph of the same memorandum Black goes on to say:

Before we can rephrase a string of words without significant loss, we must define our interests precisely. If we are interested in everything, then we cannot rephrase the string at all.

Let us say, therefore, that we are interested in assessing the possibility, and also the technical feasibility, of (1) representing large parts of the body of knowledge, as well as questions relating to the body of knowledge, in a formal language amenable to processing by a computer and (2) developing a system that will, by processing the questions and the stored corpus, deduce and display correct answers.

Black's results attest to the possibility of doing those things. However, Black's programs take a long time to determine the answers to fairly simple questions. That fact suggests that economic feasibility is dependent upon

183

greatly increasing the processing efficiency of the question-answering system or the processing speed of the computer, or both. The prediction made in Part I, that it is unlikely that there will be great increases in speed in the same computers that have a greatly increased memory capacity, may not bear very heavily on this problem. It may be that we will use procedures that are fast, but not very deep, to retrieve parts of the corpus that are rich in statements germane to a particular question, and then turn to deeper and slower procedures for the derivation of the answer from the rich informational ore.

The first of Black's two contributions to be summarized, the memorandum, "Specific-Question-Answering System," February 8, 1963, describes Version III of a system written in the LISP language for the IBM 7090 computer (McCarthy et al., 1962; Berkeley and Bobrow, 1964). In this system, the corpus consists of statements that are strings of ordinary words, symbols representing variables, and parentheses. The use of the ordinary words is highly constrained — so constrained that nothing can be said that could not be said equally well in the shorter, but less widely readable, notation seen in books on logic. The only variables are *X1*, *X2*, *X3*, *what, when, which,* and *how.* The parentheses have the effect of forcing the system to consider as a unit the string within the parentheses.

The "questions" asked of the Specific-Question-Answering System may be either statements, in which case they are confirmed or denied by the system, or ordinary questions containing the variables, *X1, X2, X3, what,* and *when,* etc. The answer elicited by a "yes-no" question is "yes," "no," or "no answer." The answer to any

184

other question is a list of items that constitute a correct and reasonable reply, or "no answer."

The system seeks answers to questions by processing the questions and the corpus in a very straightforward, rigorous way. It looks through the corpus for a statement that is the same as the statement that constitutes the question (in the case of questions in statement form) or that can be transformed into the question by removing a "not." If it finds a match, the answer is "yes." If it finds a negated match, the answer is "no." If it finds neither, it looks for a conditional statement in the corpus in which the consequent matches the question. If it finds such a statement in the corpus, it undertakes to determine an answer to the subsidiary question, whether or not the premise of the conditional statement is true. Proceeding in this way, it tries every possibility of deriving the question or its negation from the statements of the corpus.

The procedure for processing of questions containing variables is a little more complex than the procedure just described. It is necessary, in seeking an answer to a question containing a variable, to keep track of all the individuals (people, objects, etc.) that can be values of the variable. The process amounts, approximately, to determining the list of individuals that meet all the conditions that are imposed upon the variable.

The system is capable of answering not only simple, single-variable questions, but also multiple questions (conjunctions of simple questions), conditional questions (containing if . . . then . . .), and even questions containing the names of LISP computer programs. In the latter case, there is a rigid format that must be followed in giving the name of the program and its arguments.

185

All the foregoing structures mentioned as acceptable question forms are also acceptable as forms for statements in the corpus. In the corpus, a program name may occur even in the antecedent of a conditional statement. We mention these things to indicate that the system has the capability of expressing complex relations and of deriving answers to complex questions.

To see approximately what the system does, let us consider a few oversimplified examples and one more complex example. Suppose, first, that the corpus consists merely of two statements:

```
MERCURY IS (A PLANET)
IF (X1 IS A PLANET) THEN (X1 IS A PLANET
OF THE SUN)
```

The question asked of the system, in statement form, is:

```
MERCURY IS A PLANET OF THE SUN
```

To that question, the system says, simply:

```
YES
```

Suppose, for the second example, that the corpus consists of only one sentence:

```
EARTH IS SMALLER THAN JUPITER
```

The question asked of the system and the foregoing rudimentary corpus is:

```
JUPITER IS SMALLER THAN EARTH
```

The answer given by the system to that question is:

```
NO ANSWER
```

But now suppose that a second statement is added to the corpus. The corpus now consists of the two statements:

```
EARTH IS SMALLER THAN JUPITER
IF (X1 IS SMALLER THAN X2) THEN (X2 IS NOT
SMALLER THAN X1)
```

The question is still:

```
JUPITER IS SMALLER THAN EARTH
```

The system is now able to determine an answer. It says:

```
NO
```

This example illustrates one of the basic notions underlying Black's work: It is possible, and it may be highly
desirable, to put most of the "intelligence" of the system
into its corpus and to let the processing program itself
retain a high degree of simplicity and, if the term is appropriate, formal elegance. As will be seen, the same
notion appears in "Ontogeny," to be described later, even
though Ontogeny is approximately the antithesis of
Black's system in respect of rigor and tightness of formalization.

The final example involves a corpus consisting of eight
direct statements and three conditional statements. They
are:

```
MERCURY IS NEXT SMALLER THAN PLUTO
PLUTO IS NEXT SMALLER THAN MARS
MARS IS NEXT SMALLER THAN VENUS
VENUS IS NEXT SMALLER THAN EARTH
EARTH IS NEXT SMALLER THAN NEPTUNE
NEPTUNE IS NEXT SMALLER THAN URANUS
URANUS IS NEXT SMALLER THAN SATURN
SATURN IS NEXT SMALLER THAN JUPITER
IF (X1 IS NEXT SMALLER THAN X2) THEN
   (X1 IS SMALLER THAN X2)
IF (X1 IS NEXT SMALLER THAN X2) AND
   (X2 IS SMALLER THAN X3) THEN
   (X1 IS SMALLER THAN X3)
IF (EARTH IS SMALLER THAN X1) THEN
   (X1 IS A MAJOR PLANET)
```

187

The question asked of the system and this corpus is:

WHAT IS A MAJOR PLANET

The answer provided by the system is:

NEPTUNE
URANUS
SATURN
JUPITER

This last example would be more impressive than it is if the corpus contained a large number of irrelevant statements in addition to the statements shown. The presence of irrelevant statements would increase the length of time required by the computer in answering the question, but the computer has the great advantage, in operations of this kind, that it does not tend to forget the relevant facts already found while it is examining the irrelevancies. For a human being, on the other hand, a problem of the present kind that is difficult but nevertheless within one's scope of capability becomes entirely hopeless as soon as a large amount of irrelevant material is introduced. That fact, we believe, is significant in its bearing on the problem men face in drawing answers from the body of knowledge that is now held in libraries and document rooms.

The other paper of Black's that we shall discuss here is "A Question-Answering System: QAS-5" (1963). This paper describes in detail the operation of a later-generation question-answering system, a descendant of the Specific-Question-Answering System that we have been discussing. The main advances made in the interim between the two papers were advances in the handling of quantification and advances achieved by formalizing the language approximately in a way suggested earlier by McCarthy (1959). The advance in quantification makes it possible for the system to deal with problems involving "some" and "all." The formalization of the language makes it difficult for the uninitiated reader to understand what is being done, but it reveals the flaws and pitfalls to the veteran in a clearer way than the more readable language does, and, moreover, it suggests what to do to correct or avoid them. We consider the formalization, therefore, to be a step more in a right direction than in a wrong one — a step that must be taken in order to reach a position from which it will be possible to move forward to simultaneous readability and formal effectiveness.

The mode of operation of QAS-5 is similar in basic principle, though somewhat deeper and more complex, to the mode of operation of the Specific-Question-Answering System. Some of the flavor of the method is given by the following protocol:

Step 1: The system finds the first match for question 1 in statement 6.

Step 2: The system forms the backward transform of question 1 and statement 6, giving a new conditional (7) — at (desk, y), at (y, country) → at (desk, country).

Step 3: The system sets up the first antecedent of (7) as a new question (2) — at (desk, y).

Step 4: The system finds the first match for question 2 in statement 2.

Step 5: The system forms the transform of question 2 and statement 2, giving the answer to question 2 — (I) at (desk, home).

The latter would be read, as one might possibly guess, "I am at my desk at home."

The problem to which Black's QAS-5 report is wholly

dedicated is a problem posed by McCarthy in 1958 and hitherto not solved by any nonhuman system. It is a well known problem in artificial-intelligence and heuristic-programming circles and is called the "airport problem." The problem, stated here informally, is fairly simple:

I am at my desk, at home. My car is in my garage, which is also at my home. I want to go to the airport. The airport is in the same county as my home. I can walk from any point that I would call "at my home" to any other point that I would also call "at my home," because, of course, the dimensions of the area subsumed under "home" are not very great. I can drive from any point in my county to any other point in my county. What should I do?

The answer to the question, or the solution to the problem, is said to be:

I should go from my desk to my garage on foot and get my car, and I should then drive my car from the garage to the airport.

Having stated the problem and given the solution, we should perhaps repeat that, although the answer is obvious to any adult human being who understands English, no one had succeeded in devising a wholly automatic system that would derive the answer (or a formal statement corresponding to the answer) from the description of the situation and the statement of the question (or formalizations of them). Black's report gives a step-by-step account of the procedure used by QAS-5 in solving the problem. In addition, it displays, point by point, the minor differences between the notation suggested by McCarthy and the notation employed by Black.

The conclusions that we draw from our experience with question-answering systems are summed up in the assertion that the achievement of Black's program in

190

solving McCarthy's problem is simultaneously a signal advance in automated question answering and a commonplace performance for a moderate intelligence. In greater detail, the conclusions are:

1. Clear progress is being made in bringing logical deduction within the scope of automation.

2. In the process of programming a system to accomplish a feat such as the one described, one begins to see how extremely deep and complex are the intellectual processes that one accepts as commonplace and undemanding of intelligence when those processes are carried out by people.

3. In the running of such programs, one begins to sense the magnitude of the gulf that separates a demonstration of the type just described from an economically feasible operating system. As the problems become more complex, and as the corpus becomes larger, the amount of time required for processing goes up steeply. This is a discouraging counterpoise to the pattern of growth of the information-processing technology described in Part I.

4. At the same time, one sees, even at this stage, many ways in which processing can be made more efficient, and one senses that there are — waiting to be discovered — ways of formulating the procedure that are much more powerful than the ways thus far employed.

In short, it appears to us that the domain of question-answering systems is an intellectually deep and technologically demanding area for research and development. As suggested, there is an extremely long way to go before useful answers can be deduced from extensive information bases at reasonable cost. On the other hand, it may well be that, in this area, each basic conceptual advance will be a long stride toward the procognitive systems we envision for man's future interaction with the fund of knowledge.

AN APPROACH TO COMPUTER PROCESSING OF NATURAL LANGUAGE

This final project was pursued intensively during the first year of the study, but, for reasons not related to its degree of promise, it lay dormant during the second year. Although the project does not appear to be worth continuing in its present form, the following description may prove useful.

The approach selected at the outset — to try to mirror in computer programs the ontogenetic development of the human ability to generate and understand language — was quite different from the approach, then more popular, based upon syntactic analysis. The approach adopted paid more attention to semantics than to syntax. However, many of the investigators who earlier had concentrated on syntactic analysis have directed their efforts toward semantic analysis, and what seemed to us at the outset to be an unpopulated field is rapidly becoming crowded. That fact, together with our sharpening awareness of the very great difficulty and even greater extent of the task, account for the negativeness of our thoughts about reactivating "Ontogeny."

At the beginning of the project, it seemed to us to be a good idea to start with "baby talk" and to try to recapitulate, as closely as possible, the development of the human language process. Recognizing the importance of the "verbal community" in each individual's development

192

of language process, we set up a situation in which an operator at the typewriter played the role of the verbal community and, acting as stimulator, instructor, reinforcer, umpire, and protector, presided over the "shaping up" of language behavior in the computer.

It was necessary, of course, to provide the computer with basic structures and capabilities corresponding roughly to those that would be inherited by a human being. It was necessary also to set up some domain of discourse that would be potentially "meaningful" to the computer, as well as to the operator, and that would provide an analogue to the "environment" in which human beings behave and with reference to which most of their language — that is not about themselves — is oriented.

One part of the internal mechanism — of the system of computer programs — seems worth describing despite the fact that its nature does not in any direct way determine the nature of the over-all system. This part of the program is concerned with the representation, in the computer memory, of the words and phrases communicated between the operator and the computer. In the input and output equipment, the words and phrases take the form of strings of characters or character codes. The codes are the so-called "concise" codes for alphanumeric characters employed in the PDP-1 computer. Each code is a pattern of six binary digits.

Representation of words, phrases, and so forth, as strings of coded characters is inconvenient and uneconomical for many information-processing purposes. In a computing machine that has registers of fixed length, it is inconvenient to have words and phrases of variable length. We were at the outset not so much concerned with economy of representation as with convenience of processing, and we adopted an approach designed mainly for convenience. We represented each word, or phrase, or sentence, or string of any recognized class, by a 36-bit code. The code was made up of a 30-bit main code and 6 bits of auxiliary information, which included designation of the class to which the string belonged. A 36-bit code can be stored conveniently in two consecutive registers of the PDP-1 memory.

The rule for representing incoming words in the computer memory was the following. If the word consisted of five characters or fewer, the concise-code representation (filled out with the six auxiliary bits and with "filler characters" if necessary to make it come to a total length of 36-bits) is the computer representation; if, on the other hand, the word contained more than five characters, then the computer representation consists of the concise codes of the first three characters, the six auxiliary bits, and, in addition, a 12-bit "hash code" calculated by a rather complicated procedure from the concise codes of the remaining characters. This representation is capable of discriminating among about 4000 different words with the same three leading characters. Because the calculation of the hash code is carried out by a procedure akin to the generation of "random numbers," one cannot be entirely sure that two different words will not yield the same code. Nevertheless, he can make the probability of a "collision" as low as he likes by selecting a sufficiently long representation.

In the initial stages of the work, we were not much concerned about accidental confusion of one word with another. Children certainly confuse words. Indeed, we were attracted by the hypothesis that some of the confusions that arise in human communication and thinking are attributable to something like a hash-code process in neural representation.

The agent that converts strings of text into hash codes is, of course, a computer program. First it divides a string of text into words and determines a code for each word. Then it combines the words into phrases, using punctuation as a guide, and determines a hash code for each phrase from the codes for the words within the phrase. Then it determines a hash code for each sentence from the codes for the phrases within the sentence, and so forth. Thus, for each word, for each phrase, for each sentence, . . . , there is a 36-bit representation. After the conversion to this internal code has been effected, and until a stage is reached at which it is necessary to generate a response in the form of a string of alphanumeric characters, all the processing is carried out with the internal 36-bit codes.

It is easy to transform alphanumeric text into internal codes. To do that, it is necessary only to apply the transformation programs that calculate the codes. However, to transform in the other direction — to go from the internal code representation to a string of alphanumeric characters — is another matter. Because information is sometimes lost in the forward transformation, it is not possible simply to calculate the reverse transformation. It is necessary to employ a "table-searching" procedure. However, it is certainly neither necessary nor desirable to store every string of characters received in order to have it ready to type as a response. If one is to respond in a natural way, he must be able to generate sequences of words that he has never received. Moreover, there are too many strings of words to consider storing them all in a computer memory. The procedure adopted, therefore, is to associate with each internal word code, but not with the code for any string of any class other than word, its complete concise code, i.e., the string of concise codes corresponding to the characters of the word.

The association is achieved in the following way. All the internal codes, for words, phrases, sentences, and so forth, are kept together — along with other information — in a table called the "Hash Table." One of the entries in the Hash Table, for each word represented in that table, is the address of the register in the Vocabulary Table in which the corresponding concise-code representation begins. That makes it possible, given the internal code corresponding to a word, to find the corresponding concise code and to have the word typed on the computer typewriter.

For those internally represented strings that are not merely words, there is still another table, called the "Subaddress Table." The entry in the Hash Table that is associated with a sentence the way the Vocabulary Table address is associated with a word, is the address of a register in the Subaddress Table. At that address in the Subaddress Table, one finds the beginning of a list of "subaddresses" that are addresses of registers back in the Hash Table. In those registers in the Hash Table are the entries for strings of the next lower class. (Since this example started with a sentence, they are entries for phrases.) With each hash code for a phrase is associated the address of another register in the Subaddress Table. Going back to the Subaddress Table with that address, one finds addresses of registers in the Hash Table. Finally, in the designated registers in the Hash Table are addresses of registers in the Vocabulary Table. In the Vocabulary Table, of course, are the concise codes of the words.

The procedure just described is implemented by programming, so no effort of thought is involved after the program has been perfected. The program runs much more rapidly than the typewriter can type, and there is therefore no observable delay. With the system, one can start out with a 36-bit hash code and wind up with a long typewritten sentence. If the initial code is the code of a paragraph, indeed he winds up with a paragraph. We have checked the system to that level of operation. Obviously, nothing stands in the way of representing an entire book with a 36-bit internal code. However, one cannot uniquely represent the individuals of any set of size approaching 2^n with hash codes n bits in length. Our selection of 36-bit codes, and our compromise in the direction of readability by man as well as by machine, was conditioned by the fact that we were working with a "young" language mechanism that would not be expected to develop a very large vocabulary for some time.

It is now doubtless evident that a description of computer programs in ordinary language encounters serious problems of exposition and endurance. We shall, therefore, not describe the entire Ontogeny program in as great detail. Let us, nevertheless, explain how the system is designed to keep track of the properties of the various words and phrases and the entities and operations for which they stand.

The repository for factual information, in Ontogeny, is a table called the "Property Table." One of the entries in each section of the Hash Table is the address of a corresponding section in the Property Table. For convenience, the Property Table records the corresponding Hash Table address and also the internal code of the string with which the properties are associated. The properties themselves are represented by internal codes. When it is necessary to determine the meanings of the property codes, one has to find the codes in the Hash Table and go on from there in the way just described.

The structure within which properties are represented in the Property Table is a simple hierarchy, an "outline." The rules for listing properties are loose. In the main, they were made up as problems arose, and indeed a certain amount of care was taken *not* to create a sharp, formal, rigid system. Syntactic and semantic properties are mixed indiscriminately. In the basic system, there is not even any distinction between the symbol and the thing for which it stands. That is to say, under "table" we might record the property of being used mainly as a noun, the property of being used sometimes as a verb, and the property of usually being made of wood. The representation of this last property may take the form:

```
table
    material
        wood
            usually
        steel
            sometimes
```

However, the system would be expected to function without great difficulty if, through happenstance, the arrangement were set up as:

```
table
    material
        usually
            wood
        sometimes
            steel
```

We did not reach the point at which programs actually operated with that kind of irregularity of format, but we did have search programs that examined the "next level down" if they did not find a satisfactory property on the level initially assigned.

From the description thus far, it may be evident that the Property Table is, by nature, full of circular definitions. Everything is defined in terms of something else — except for a relatively few primitives that are associated with subroutines. One of the properties of "move," for example, is that move is often used as a verb. Another is that, when it is so used, it is to be implemented by executing a subroutine that is capable of taking arguments that answer "what," "by whom," "from where," and "to where." Some of the properties of "pencil" refer to its capability of serving as an argument. A pencil is "movable," "takable," "bringable," and so forth.

We are now almost in a position to turn our attention to the procedure through which an incoming message is processed and responded to by the computer. One more part of the system must be described, however, before that can be done conveniently. This remaining part is the one that has to do with the "domain of discourse" mentioned earlier.

The domain of discourse is a model room equipped with a few items of furniture. The room has a door that can be opened to various degrees, a window that can be opened or closed, a table that can occupy any otherwise unoccupied position within the room, and a chair subject to the same constraint. There are a book and a pencil, to be manipulated, an active agent called "Comp," and another active agent called "Oper." The discourse involves Comp and Oper and is actually carried out by the computer and the operator.

The room and its contents are represented in the computer memory, of course, and they are also represented diagrammatically by simple line drawings on the screen of the oscilloscope. When the door is opened, the representation of the door in the computer memory changes, and the schematic door on the oscilloscope screen (a straight line with a little figure near one end representing the door knob) swings.

The basic subroutines, corresponding to operations in the domain of discourse, are implementations of "move," "go," "carry," "bring," "open," "close," "put," etc. These subroutines, together with the subroutines that handle the encoding and decoding, the search for properties and the analysis of input messages, were all that we actually prepared and operated. The plan encompassed two additional classes of subroutines. The first of these was to handle the addition, deletion and modification of properties, under the control of input messages. The second was to handle the addition and modification of subroutines, again under the control of input messages. If we had been able to carry through to some accomplishments in the first additional category, we should have been able to increase the verbal capability of the system, but only by adding to its knowledge — to its vocabulary and its fund of facts. If we had been able to move on into the second additional category, we should have had within our grasp the capability of achieving almost unlimited restructuring and reorganization of the system. But we did not accomplish either of those things, and we mention them here only to indicate that the approach had a higher aspiration than merely to move line diagrams about on the screen of an oscilloscope.

Now, at last, we come to the procedure employed in analyzing the incoming messages and selecting and directing the actions taken in response to them. The responses were, as suggested earlier, to move things about in the room, to make replies by way of the typewriter, and — in hope but not in actuality — to add to the internally stored knowledge and to the internally stored behavior patterns. By knowledge, of course, we mean the contents of the several tables mentioned earlier. By behavior patterns, we mean the set of subroutines available for use in responding.

The problem of interpreting an incoming message is, in the approach we have been describing, to select the appropriate subroutine or patterns of subroutines and to find the arguments that they require under the prevailing circumstances. The selection of subroutines is guided by associating subroutines with verbs. The search is carried out by a part of the program that examines the internal codes that represent the incoming message and a list of roles that the message segments may play. Records are kept in a matrix during the processing of a message. The rows of the matrix are associated with the words of the incoming message. The columns of the matrix are associated with the possible roles.

In the version of Ontogeny that was carried to the point of demonstration, the processing deals only with words.

The first step is to look up each word of the incoming message in the Property Table and place a tally in each cell of the matrix that corresponds to a function that the word can fulfill. When this has been done for all the words of the message, the task becomes one of finding an appropriate and consistent assignment of words to functions and, at the same time, a correspondence between the functions and the argument requirements of a subroutine that goes with the verb.

The procedure used to carry out this task starts by "freezing" the rows and columns of the matrix that contain only a single tally. The next step is to prepare simpler matrix patterns in which each of the words at first associated with two or more roles is assigned to a single role. These simpler matrixes are then considered one at a time.

The subroutines corresponding to the word assigned to the verb category in the first simplified matrix are examined. If one of them has a set of argument requirements that match the roles to which words are assigned, then that subroutine is selected, the arguments are supplied to it, and the response is executed. In an effort to get the system into operation quickly, we satisfied ourselves with the first subroutine that met the requirements. If no subroutine met the requirements of the first assignment pattern, the second assignment pattern was used, and so on. As soon as a suitable subroutine was found, supplied with arguments, and executed, the response was considered accomplished. The program then simply went into a "listening" mode and waited for the operator to take the next step.

Toward the end of the work on Ontogeny, we were planning a set of subroutines that would operate on higher-echelon strings than words. With this set of subroutines, there was to be associated a subsystem for keeping track, in a primitive way, of the "situation." The system was to be capable of asking, on receipt of a message, "Am I already familiar with this message in this context?" If so, it was to inquire of itself what response it had previously made and how effective the response had been. If the result had been sufficiently favorable, then — according to the plan — the system would simply have made the same response again and taken notes on its effect.

In the likely event that no record existed of previous experience with the over-all message in the prevailing context, then the projected system would work with lower-echelon segments of the message, hoping to find that one or more of them was already "understood." In the absence of usable prior experience at each echelon, the system would drop down to the next-lower echelon until it finally came to words. Failing to understand a word, or failing to understand a phrase given experience with the words of the phrase, it would ask for help.

Our experience with Ontogeny left us with five main impressions: (1) It seems possible, and even likely, that we could store up enough substantive information in a computer memory to handle the analysis of natural language — semantic as well as syntactic — an analysis capable of supporting "reasonable" responses, if only the domain of discourse is not very wide. (2) It is probably more important to limit the domain of discourse than to limit the length or complexity of the input messages. (3) Many so-called semantic properties play roles that are almost indistinguishable from syntactic roles. The distinction between things that are capable of acting with initiative as voluntary agents and things that are not, for example, seems to be approximately as important as the

203

distinction between the active voice and the passive voice of verbs. (4) A sympathetic, cooperative, verbal, community is a fundamental essential for the development of a sophisticated verbal mechanism. To develop complex language behavior in a neutral environment would, we think, take another long-suffering recapitulation of evolution. (5) On the other hand, no one seems likely to design or invent a formal system capable of automating sophisticated language behavior. The best approach, therefore, seems to us to be somewhere between the extremes — to call for a formal base plus an overlay of experience gained in interaction with the cooperative verbal community.

References

ANDREYEV, N. D., Linguistic Aspects of Translation. Proceedings of the Ninth International Congress of Linguistics, Cambridge, Mass., 1962.

BEMER, R. W., Do it by the Numbers—Digital Shorthand. *Communications of the Association for Computing Machinery,* **3,** 530–536, 1960.

BERKELEY, E. C., and D. G. BOBROW (Eds.), The Programming Language LISP: Its Operation and Applications. Information International, Inc., Cambridge, Mass., March 1964.

BLACK, F. S., A Question-Answering System: QAS-5. Report 1063, Bolt Beranek and Newman Inc., Cambridge, Mass., October 1963.

BOBROW, D. G., Syntactic Analysis of English by Computer—A Survey. *Proceedings of the American Federation of Information Processing Societies,* **24,** 365–387, 1963. (Based on Report 1055, Bolt Beranek and Newman Inc., Cambridge, Mass., August 1963.)

BOBROW, D. G., R. Y. KAIN, B. RAPHAEL, and J. C. R. LICKLIDER, A Computer-Program System to Facilitate the Study of Technical Documents. Report 1103, Bolt Beranek and Newman Inc., Cambridge, Mass., November 1963. (To be published in *American Documentation.*)

BOURNE, C. P., The World's Technical Journal Literature: An Estimate of Volume, Origin, Language, Field, Indexing, and Abstracting. Stanford Research Institute, Menlo Park, Calif., November 1961.

CHOMSKY, N., Three Models for the Description of Language. *IRE Transactions on Information Theory,* **IT-2** (3), 113–124, 1956.

CHOMSKY, N., *Syntactic Structures.* Mouton, S'Gravenhage, 1957.

CLAPP, L. C., Associative Chaining as an Information-Retrieval Technique. Report 1079, Bolt Beranek and Newman Inc., Cambridge, Mass., 1963.

GIULIANO, V. E., Analogue Networks for Word Association. *IEEE Transactions on Military Electronics,* MIL-7, Nos. 2, 3, April–July 1963, 221–234.

GIULIANO, V. E., and P. E. JONES, Linear Associative Information Retrieval. In P. Howerton (Ed.), *Vistas in Information Handling.* Spartan Press, Baltimore, Md., 1963.

GREEN, B. F., A. K. WOLF, C. CHOMSKY, and K. LAUGHERY, Baseball: An Automatic Question-Answerer. *Proceedings of the Western Joint Computer Conference,* **19,** 219–224, 1961.

GRIGNETTI, M., On the Length of a Class of Serial Files. Report 1011, Bolt Beranek and Newman Inc., Cambridge, Mass., June 1963a. (Submitted for publication in *American Documentation.*)

GRIGNETTI, M., Computer Aids to Literature Searches. Report 1074, Bolt Beranek and Newman Inc., Cambridge, Mass., November 1963b.

GRIGNETTI, M., A Note on the Entropy of Words in Printed English. *Information and Control,* **7,** 304–306, 1964. (Based on Report 1073, Bolt Beranek and Newman Inc., Cambridge, Mass., October 1963.)

GROSS, M., On the Equivalence Models of Language Used in the Fields of Mechanical Translation and Information Retrieval. Memorandum, Mechanical Translation Group, Massachusetts Institute of Technology, Cambridge, Mass., 1962.

HARRIS, Z. S., String Analysis of Sentence Structure. Mouton, The Hague, 1962.

HAYS, D. G., Automatic Language-Data Processing. In H. Borko (Ed.), *Computer Applications in the Behavioral Sciences.* Prentice-Hall, New York, 1962, pp. 394–423.

KLEIN, S., Automatic Decoding of Written English. Ph.D. Thesis, University of California, Berkeley, Calif., 1963.

KLEIN, S., and R. F. SIMMONS, A Computational Approach to Grammatical Coding of English Words. *Journal of the Association for Computing Machinery,* **10,** 334–347, 1963.

KUNO, S., and A. G. OETTINGER, Syntactic Structure and Ambiguity of English. *Proceedings of the 1963 Fall Joint Computer Conference.* Spartan Books, Baltimore, Md., 1963, pp. 397–418.

LICKLIDER, J. C. R., Panel Discussion on Man-Machine Interaction. Gordon Research Conference on Information Problems in Research, South Hampton, New Hampshire, July 3, 1962.

LICKLIDER, J. C. R., and W. E. CLARK, On-Line Man-Computer Communication. *Proceedings of the American Federation of Information Processing Societies,* **21,** 113–128, 1962.

LINDSAY, R. K., Inferential Memory as the Basis of Machines Which Understand Natural Language. In E. Feigenbaum and J. Feldman (Eds.), *Computers and Thought.* McGraw-Hill, New York, 1963, pp. 217–233.

MARILL, T., Libraries and Question-Answering Systems. Report 1071, Bolt Beranek and Newman Inc., Cambridge, Mass., November 1963.

MCCARTHY, J., Programs with Common Sense. *Proceedings of Symposium on Mechanization of Thought Processes.* Vol. I. Her Majesty's Stationery Office, London, 1959, pp. 77–84.

MCCARTHY, J., P. W. ABRAHAMS, D. J. EDWARDS, T. P. HART, and M. I. LEVIN, *LISP 1.5 Programmer's Manual.* The M.I.T. Press, Cambridge, Mass., 1962.

MOLOSHNAVA, T. N., An Algorithm for Translating from the English to the Russian [Translated from the Russian]. *Foreign Developments in Machine Translation and Information Processing,* No. 11, 1–40, December 29, 1960. (Available from the Office of Technical Services, U.S. Department of Commerce; and as JPRS 6492, U.S. Joint Publication Research Service, Washington, D. C.)

207

OETTINGER, A. G., and S. KUNO, Multiple-Path Syntactic Analyzer. *Proceedings of the International Federation of Information Processing Congress—1962.* Munich, 1962.

OSGOOD, C. E., G. J. SUCI, and P. TANNENBAUM, *The Measurement of Meaning.* University of Illinois Press, Urbana, 1957.

RHODES, I., A New Approach to the Mechanical Syntactical Analysis of Russian. *Mechanical Translation,* **6,** 33–50, 1961.

ROBINSON, J. J., Preliminary Codes and Rules for Automatic Parsing of English. Research Memorandum RM3339, Rand Corporation, Santa Monica, Calif., December 1962.

SENDERS, J. W., Information Storage Requirements for the Contents of the World's Libraries. *Science,* **141,** 1067–1068, 1963.

SWANSON, R., Word Correlation and Automatic Indexing. Reports C82-9U9, C82-OU1, Ramo Wooldridge Corp., Canoga Park, Calif., 1959.

SWETS, J. A., Information Retrieval Systems, *Science,* **141,** 245–250, 1963. (Based on Measures of Effectiveness of Information-Retrieval Systems. Report 982, Bolt Beranek and Newman Inc., Cambridge, Mass., 1963.)

THOMPSON, F. B., The Semantic Interface in Man-Machine Communication. Report RM 63TMP-35, General Electric Company, Santa Barbara, Calif., 1963.

WALKER, D. E., and J. M. BARTLETT, The Structure of Languages for Man and Computer: Problems in Formalization. Paper presented at the First Congress of the Information Sciences, Hot Springs, Va., 1962. (Sponsored by Mitre Corporation, Burlington, Mass.)

WEIZENBAUM, J., Symmetric List Processor. *Communications of the Association for Computing Machinery,* **6,** 524–544, 1963.

WILLIAMS, T. M., R. F. BARNES, and J. W. KUIPERS, Discussion of Major Features of a Restricted Logistic Grammar for Topic Representation. Report 5206-26, Itek Laboratory, Waltham, Mass., 1962.

Index

Abrahams, P. W., 207
Abstract, 7, 51, 53, 55, 58, 106, 175
Abstracting, 5
Access, 16–19
  multiple, 68
  random, 8, 16, 17, 62, 68
Access time, 16, 18
Acoustical Society of America, viii
Acquisition
  of information, 37, 38
  of knowledge, 21–26, 28
Acquisition policy, 38
ADAM, 67
Advisory Committee, xi, xii
Aims of procognitive systems, 21, 31–32
Airport problem, 190
Alfred P. Sloan Foundation, vii
ALGOL, 66, 123, 159
Algorithm, 55, 81, 91, 113, 114, 180–182, 209
Alphanumeric character, 7, 13–15, 24, 97, 99, 100, 121–123, 132, 144, 166, 193–196

Alphanumeric information, 25, 114, 166
Analysis
  constituent, 140
  dependency, 134
  discontinuous-constituent, 138
  hierarchical, 73
  immediate-constituent, 134–136
  of knowledge, 21, 44, 60
  phrase-structure, 134
  predictive, 136
  relational, 82
  semantic, 54, 56, 192, 203
  syntactic, 54, 56, 68, 116, 129, 131–133, 140, 141, 192, 203
  transformational, 140
Analytical semantics, 61
Andreyev, N. D., 134
Application
  of information, 37
  of knowledge, 24, 26–28, 31, 35, 67, 112, 150
Application system, 27
APT, 67

209

210

Communication mode, 121–124
Communication pool, 165–166
Compiler of programs, 50, 159, 160
Compiling of programs, 51
Compression code, 147
Computer
  Atlas, 169
  PDP-1, 158, 193, 194
  7090, 184
Computer-aided learning, 170
Computer-aided teaching, 127, 170
Computer-facilitated study, 127, 177
Computer instruction, 19, 29–31, 49,
    65, 107, 115, 122, 160, 161,
    165, 171–174
Computer memory, 9, 15–18, 25, 26,
    38, 41, 43, 45, 53, 58, 62–64,
    67, 79–81, 102, 104, 106, 121,
    132, 144, 147, 158, 168, 171,
    173, 184, 193, 194, 200, 203
Computer processor, 6, 9, 15, 19, 38,
    42, 58, 65, 163, 171; see also
    Processing of information
Computer program, 8, 29, 35, 39,
    50, 57, 58, 66, 84, 85, 92, 94,
    104, 107–112, 115, 121, 123,
    125, 129, 132, 134, 136, 137,
    140, 158, 160, 163, 165, 166,
    168, 170–177, 180, 181, 185–
    187, 192, 193, 195, 197, 199
Computer-program model, 111
Computer programmer, 104, 105,
    107–110, 119, 121, 162–166
Computer programming, 48–51, 58,
    65, 104, 125, 158, 160, 166,
    176, 182, 191, 197
  heuristic, 190
Computer science, 60
Computer system
  multiple-access, 68
  multiple-console, 42
Concise code, 193, 194, 196, 197
Concordance, 181
Console, 33, 41, 46–48, 52, 69, 92–
    94, 96, 100–103, 105, 113,
    120, 127
Constituent analysis, 140
Content-addressable memory, 8, 64,
    65
Content word, 132
Control of computers, 41, 47–49, 51,
    57, 66, 67, 92, 97, 98, 101,
    103, 113, 120, 122, 124

Control language, 114, 122
Control mode, 121–124
Control station, 33
Conversation between man and
    computer, 36, 124, 125
Coordinate index, 74, 75, 143, 181
Core memory; see Memory, mag-
    netic-core
Corpus, 9, 14–16, 20, 24, 25, 28, 38,
    41, 44, 61–63, 67, 68, 87,
    125, 153, 154, 179–181, 183–
    188, 191
Correlation, 55, 77, 78, 112, 117, 118
Council on Library Resources, Inc.,
    vi, vii, ix, xi, 1, 2, 100
Criterion
  of pertinence, 148, 149
  for procognitive systems, 21, 32–
    39
  for the program of study, 2
Cryogenic memory, 16, 63

Data base, 26, 31, 53, 66, 88, 89,
    114
Data structure, 112, 119
DDT, 121, 122
Debugging system, 121
DECAL, 66, 159, 160, 162, 174, 175
Decision theory, 150
Decoding, 143, 146, 147, 200
Defense, Department of, viii
Defense Documentation Center, 74
Delay-line memory, 16
Delimiter, 181
Dependency analysis, 134
Dependency grammar, 132
Descriptor, 7, 45, 48, 50, 54, 55, 64,
    69, 70, 74, 142
Descriptor structure, 54, 55
Desk, 6, 9, 33
Dewey Decimal Classification Sys-
    tem, 61
Dictionary, 68, 132
Digital code, 39, 46, 52, 65, 73, 96,
    99, 106, 107, 144–147, 161–
    163, 178, 193–195
Digital Equipment Corporation, 158
Digital memory, 17, 18, 142–144
Direct file; see File
Discontinuous-constituent analysis,
    138
Discontinuous-constituent grammar,
    137

217